CYBERSECURITY SOLUTION

Embracing Technologies in CyberSecurity

JOHN DOLLAR

Copyright © 2024
by
John dollar

Table of Contents

INTRODUCTION

Once upon a time, in the sprawling metropolis of Cyberburg, where neon lights danced on the edges of skyscrapers and the hum of technology filled the air, there lived a brilliant young engineer named Alex Knight. Alex had always been fascinated by the digital world and the limitless possibilities it offered, but as the city's dependence on technology grew, so did the threats lurking in the shadows.

One day, Alex came across a secret document that revealed a sinister plot to launch a devastating cyberattack on Cyberburg. Determined to protect the city, Alex has assembled a team of experts, each with unique cyber security skills. Together they created "The Cyber Guardians".

Their first challenge was to develop a cutting-edge cyber security solution that could thwart the impending threat. With a razor sharp mind, Alex envisioned a revolutionary program called "SentinelShield". This advanced system was designed to harden the city's digital infrastructure, detecting potential threats in real time and neutralizing them before any damage can be done.

As the team dived into the development of SentinelShield, they faced many obstacles. The city's existing cyber security measures were outdated and vulnerable, like a crumbling fortress in the face of an impending invasion. Alex and the Guardians have worked tirelessly, pooling their expertise to create a solution that can withstand the most sophisticated cyber attacks.

With every line of code and every nightly brainstorm, SentinelShield has evolved into a formidable guardian, ready to defend Cyberburg against any digital threat. The team implemented machine learning algorithms, encryption protocols and behavioral analysis to stay one step ahead of potential attackers.

As the day of the planned cyber attack approached, the city was still blissfully unaware of the impending danger. However, the Cyber Guardians were on high alert. They monitored the city's digital landscape, watching for any unusual activity that might signal the start of an attack.

The fateful day finally arrived. The city awoke to chaos as a cyber attack unfolded and spread like wildfire across digital networks. Panic ensued as critical systems faltered and the citizens of Cyberburg were thrown into a state of uncertainty. Amidst the chaos, the Cyber Guardians activated the SentinelShield. The program came to life and unleashed its advanced algorithms and defenses against the malicious attack. It was a digital battle of epic proportions, where lines of code clashed across a vast expanse of virtual battlefield.

Driven by their determination to protect their city, the Guardians fought tirelessly against an unseen enemy. They adapted SentinelShield on the fly, tweaking its parameters and deploying countermeasures to neutralize the ever-evolving threat. As the battle raged, the city's fate hung in the balance.

Just when all hope seemed lost, SentinelShield identified a vulnerability in the attacker's code. He exploited this weakness with surgical precision and dismantled the malicious program piece by piece. The Cyber Guardians watched in triumph as the tide turned and the digital onslaught came to an abrupt halt.

The city of Cyberburg, saved from the brink of disaster, erupted in cheers as its digital heartbeat stabilized. The Cyber Guardians, the unsung heroes of the digital realm, have triumphed over the forces that sought to disrupt the fragile balance of their interconnected world.

As word of their triumph spread, Alex and the Cyber Guardians became legends in Cyberburg. SentinelShield, the sentinel they created, stood as a symbol of innovation and resilience in the face of adversity. City leaders have recognized the importance of investing in cybersecurity and ensuring that Cyberburg remains secure in an ever-evolving digital environment.

And so the story of the Cyber Guardians has become a beacon of hope, reminding the people of Cyberburg that with ingenuity, determination, and the right cybersecurity solutions, they can overcome any challenge in the vast and ever-expanding realm of the digital frontier.

Cybersecurity solutions play a key role in protecting the digital landscape from an ever-evolving array of threats. In today's connected world, where data is the lifeblood of organizations and individuals alike, the need for robust cybersecurity measures has never been more critical. This comprehensive survey delves into the multifaceted field of cybersecurity solutions, revealing the intricate web of technologies, strategies, and practices that together form a bulwark against cyber threats.

At its core, cybersecurity is a dynamic field that is constantly adapting to the changing cyber threat landscape. As technology advances, so do the methods used by malicious actors seeking unauthorized access, data breaches, and system compromises. The field of cybersecurity solutions is therefore a dynamic ecosystem of tools and techniques designed to detect, prevent, and mitigate these threats. From traditional antivirus software to cutting-edge machine learning algorithms, the arsenal of cybersecurity solutions reflects the ongoing battle between security professionals and cyber adversaries.

One of the fundamental elements of any cyber security solution is risk management. Understanding the risks associated with a particular digital environment is essential to tailoring an effective defense strategy. Threat intelligence, vulnerability assessment, and penetration testing are integral components that inform organizations of potential vulnerabilities and help them prioritize and allocate resources effectively. In this light, cybersecurity solutions become not just reactive measures, but proactive shields that anticipate and neutralize threats before they can manifest.

Encryption is a cornerstone of cybersecurity, ensuring the confidentiality and integrity of data as it travels across networks. As data becomes an increasingly valuable commodity, protecting it from unauthorized access is paramount. Encryption algorithms, secure communication protocols and cryptographic key management are central to the arsenal of cybersecurity solutions and form an impenetrable barrier against eavesdropping and unauthorized data manipulation.

Identity and Access Management (IAM) is emerging as another critical aspect of cybersecurity solutions. In a digital environment where user identities are the gateway to sensitive information, ensuring the right individuals have appropriate access rights is critical. Multi-factor authentication, biometric recognition and robust access control form a barrier against unauthorized access and reduce the likelihood of a breach due to compromised credentials.

The rise of cloud computing has transformed the traditional IT environment and brought new challenges and opportunities for cybersecurity. Cloud security solutions have become indispensable in protecting data stored and processed in cloud environments. From secure access control to encryption protocols tailored for cloud infrastructures, these solutions address the unique vulnerabilities associated with decentralized data storage and processing.

Intrusion detection and prevention systems (IDPS) represent a proactive layer within a cyber security solution. These systems continuously monitor network and system activities, identifying and responding to potential security incidents in real time. Machine learning algorithms increase the effectiveness of IDPS by learning and adapting to emerging threat patterns, providing a dynamic defense mechanism against an ever-expanding array of cyber threats.

The proliferation of Internet of Things (IoT) devices brings a new dimension to cybersecurity challenges. As connected devices permeate homes, businesses and critical infrastructure, securing the IoT ecosystem becomes a must. IoT cybersecurity solutions include device authentication, secure communication protocols, and real-time monitoring to detect and thwart potential breaches originating from vulnerable smart devices.

The human element remains both a vulnerability and a key line of defense in cybersecurity. Security training and education are an integral part of cyber security solutions, enabling individuals to recognize and mitigate potential threats. Social engineering attacks, phishing attempts, and other tactics that exploit human vulnerability underscore the importance of a comprehensive approach that addresses both the technological and human aspects of cybersecurity.

Compliance adds another layer of complexity to the cybersecurity landscape. As governments and industry create frameworks to ensure the protection of sensitive information, cybersecurity solutions must conform to these standards. From GDPR in Europe to HIPAA in healthcare, compliance with regulatory requirements is becoming a non-negotiable aspect of a cybersecurity strategy.

The field of cybersecurity solutions is a vast and interconnected ecosystem that is constantly evolving to address the ever-changing cyber threat landscape. From traditional defense mechanisms to cutting-edge technologies such as artificial intelligence and quantum-resistant cryptography, the pursuit of cybersecurity is a dynamic journey. As organizations and individuals navigate this landscape, the combination of proactive risk management, robust encryption, identity and access control, and a human-centric approach is becoming the model for a resilient cybersecurity posture. This survey aims to illuminate the multifaceted nature of cyber security solutions and offer insight into the strategies and technologies that together fortify our digital world against the relentless tide of cyber threats.

Chapter 1. Understanding the concept of Cybersecurity

Cyber security has become an integral part of our digital age as the rapid development of technology brings both opportunities and challenges. In this era of connected systems, understanding the concept of cyber security is critical to protecting sensitive information and maintaining the integrity of digital platforms. This article examines the fundamental principles of cybersecurity and delves into the importance of cybersecurity solutions in mitigating the ever-growing threats in the cyber environment.

I. Cyber Security Basics:

A. Definition and Scope:

Cybersecurity involves the practice of protecting systems, networks, and programs from digital attacks, theft, and damage. It includes a wide range of measures aimed at ensuring the confidentiality, integrity and availability of information in the digital sphere.

B. Threat landscape:

The cyber threat landscape is dynamic and multifaceted, including threats such as malware, ransomware, phishing and more. Understanding these threats is critical to developing effective cybersecurity solutions.

C. Risk Management:

Cyber security is not only about preventing attacks, but also about managing risks. Organizations need to assess potential threats, vulnerabilities and the impact of security breaches in order to implement robust risk management strategies.

II. Importance of cyber security solutions:

A. Protection of sensitive data:

One of the primary goals of a cybersecurity solution is to protect sensitive data from unauthorized access. Encryption, access control, and secure authentication mechanisms are critical components to achieving this goal.

B. Security of critical infrastructure:

As critical infrastructure becomes more dependent on digital systems, the consequences of a cyber attack can be severe. Cybersecurity solutions play a key role in protecting critical infrastructure such as power grids, transportation systems and healthcare facilities.

C. User Privacy Protection:

Cybersecurity solutions also address user privacy concerns. With the increasing amount of personal information stored online, protecting the privacy of individuals has become a key aspect of cybersecurity practices.

III. Components of effective cyber security solutions:

A. Anti-virus and anti-malware software:

These tools are essential for detecting and removing malicious software that can compromise the security of systems. Regular updates and real-time scanning contribute to their effectiveness.

B. Firewalls and Intrusion Detection Systems:

Firewalls act as barriers between a trusted internal network and untrusted external networks, while intrusion detection systems monitor network or system activities for signs of malicious behavior. Together, they provide a layered defense against cyber threats.

C. Secure Network Architecture:

Implementing secure network architectures such as Virtual Private Networks (VPNs) and Secure Socket Layer (SSL) increases the overall resilience of digital systems against cyber attacks.

IV. Challenges in implementing a cyber security solution:

A. The Evolving Nature of Threats:

The dynamic nature of cyber threats presents a challenge for cyber security solutions. Constant updates and adaptations are essential to stay ahead of emerging threats.

B. The human factor:

Human error, such as falling victim to phishing attacks or neglecting best security practices, remains a significant challenge. Cybersecurity solutions must include user education and awareness programs.

C. Resource Limitations:

Organizations often struggle with limited resources in terms of budget and qualified personnel. Balancing the need for robust cybersecurity with limited resources requires strategic planning and prioritization.

Understanding the concept of cyber security is paramount in today's digital landscape. Cybersecurity solutions are critical to protecting sensitive information, protecting user privacy, and protecting critical infrastructure. By understanding the fundamentals of cyber security and recognizing the importance of effective solutions, individuals and organizations can navigate the complex and ever-evolving world of cyber threats with resilience and vigilance.

1.1 Definition and Scope of Cybersecurity

Cybersecurity is a multidimensional field that plays a key role in protecting digital systems, networks and data from unauthorized access, attack and damage. Its scope is extensive and includes various technologies, processes and procedures aimed at protecting sensitive information and ensuring the confidentiality, integrity and availability of digital assets. In this comprehensive survey, we delve into the definition and scope of cybersecurity and highlight its importance in today's evolving cyber threat landscape.

Definition of Cybersecurity

Cybersecurity, often referred to as information security or computer security, is the practice of implementing measures to protect digital systems, networks, and data from unauthorized access, cyberattacks, and potential harm. The primary objective is to ensure the confidentiality, integrity and availability of information in the digital realm. Cybersecurity measures are designed to protect not only personal and organizational data, but also critical infrastructure, financial systems and government networks. The field of cyber security is dynamic and constantly evolving to meet emerging threats. This area addresses a wide range of security issues, including but not limited to malware, ransomware, phishing attacks, identity theft, and denial-of-service (DoS) attacks. With the increasing connectivity of devices and the ubiquitous nature of the Internet, cybersecurity has become an indispensable aspect of our digital lives.

Scope of cyber security

The scope of cyber security is vast, reflecting the diverse range of digital threats and the complex nature of modern information systems. It can be divided into several key domains, each of which deals with specific aspects of security:

1. Network Security:

- It focuses on securing the communication infrastructure and preventing unauthorized access to networks.

- Includes the implementation of firewalls, intrusion detection and prevention systems, VPNs and other measures to protect the integrity and confidentiality of data in transit.

2. Endpoint Security:

- It deals with the security of individual devices such as computers, smartphones and tablets.

- Includes the use of anti-virus software, encryption and device management policies to protect endpoints from malware and unauthorized access.

3. Application Security:

- Includes securing software applications and preventing vulnerabilities that could be exploited by attackers.

- Includes secure coding practices, regular software updates, and penetration testing to identify and remediate potential vulnerabilities.

4. Data security:

- Focuses on protecting the confidentiality and integrity of sensitive data.

- Includes encryption, access control and data loss prevention measures to ensure that information is accessible only to authorized users.

5. Cloud Security:

- Addresses security issues related to cloud computing platforms and services.

- Includes authentication, encryption and monitoring to ensure the security of cloud-hosted data and applications.

6. Incident Response and Management:

- Involves planning and executing strategies for responding to and recovering from cyber security incidents.

- Includes the creation of incident response teams, incident detection tools and recovery plans.

7. Identity and Access Management:

- Focuses on managing user identities and controlling access to digital resources.

- Includes authentication mechanisms, authorization policies and identity verification processes.

8. Safety Awareness and Training:
- Recognizes the human element in cyber security and aims to educate users on security best practices.
- Includes training programs, awareness campaigns, and simulated phishing exercises to improve organizations' cybersecurity posture.

Cyber security solutions:
Cybersecurity relies on a myriad of solutions, technologies and practices to address the various challenges within its purview. These solutions are designed to proactively defend against threats and reactively respond to incidents. Key cybersecurity solutions include:

1. Firewalls:
- Acts as a barrier between the trusted internal network and untrusted external networks,

monitoring and controlling incoming and outgoing network traffic.

2. Anti-virus and anti-malware software:

- Detects and removes malicious software, including viruses, worms and Trojan horses, from devices and networks.

3. Intrusion Detection and Prevention Systems (IDPS):

- Monitor network or system activities for malicious actions or policy violations and respond by blocking or alerting.

4. Encryption:

- Converts data into a secure format to prevent unauthorized access and ensures that even if the data is captured, it remains unreadable.

5. Multi-Factor Authentication (MFA):

- Adds another layer of security by requiring users to provide various forms of identification before accessing digital resources.

6. Security Information and Event Management (SIEM):

- Collects and analyzes security data from various sources to identify and respond to potential security threats.

7. Petra Testing:

- Simulates cyber attacks to identify vulnerabilities in systems, networks and applications, enabling organizations to proactively address vulnerabilities.

8.Safety Training and Awareness Programs:

- Educate users on cybersecurity best practices and ensure they are aware of potential threats and know how to respond.

Cyber security is an essential component of the digital age, which aims to protect information and ensure the smooth functioning of digital systems. Its definition includes a wide range of practices, technologies and processes aimed at mitigating cyber threats. The scope of cyber security includes network security, endpoint security, application security, data security, cloud security, incident response, identity management and security awareness.

The constant evolution of cyber threats requires a proactive and adaptive approach to cyber security. As technology advances, so must the solutions and strategies used to protect against emerging risks. Continued collaboration between cybersecurity professionals, organizations, and technology developers is critical to maintaining strong defenses against the ever-changing cyber threat landscape. Ultimately, cybersecurity is not just a technological effort, but a collaborative effort to secure the digital foundation upon which our modern society rests.

1.2 Evolution of Cyber Threats

The evolution of cyber threats has been a dynamic and relentless force that has shaped the landscape of cyber security solutions over the years. In the early days of computing, threats were relatively simple, often limited to isolated incidents of unauthorized access. However, as the Internet expands and technology advances, cyber threats are becoming increasingly sophisticated and pose serious challenges to individuals, businesses, and governments.

1. Dawn of Cyber Threats:
In the early stages of the Internet, cyber threats were more about individual hackers exploring vulnerabilities for personal gain or recognition. The first types of malware to appear were viruses and worms, which were spread via floppy disks and later via email. As technology has advanced, so have the tactics of cyber attackers, giving rise to more complex threats.

2. Rise of Malware and Exploits:
The late 20th century saw the rise of malware, which includes a variety of malicious software such as viruses, trojans, and ransomware. Malware has become a popular tool for cybercriminals seeking financial gain or aiming to disrupt systems. Attacks targeting software vulnerabilities were prevalent, with attackers exploiting weaknesses in operating systems and applications to compromise systems.

3. Web threats and social engineering:

The advent of the World Wide Web has brought new vectors for cyber threats. Phishing, a form of social engineering, has gained attention as attackers attempt to manipulate individuals into divulging sensitive information. Malicious websites and drive-by downloads have become common, abusing web browsers and plugins to compromise users' devices. As online activities have grown, so has the surface for potential threats.

4. Advanced Persistent Threats (APT):

In the 21st century, state-sponsored cyber espionage has emerged as a significant threat. Advanced Persistent Threats (APTs) involve highly skilled and organized attackers, often backed by governments, targeting specific entities for intelligence gathering or sabotage. These attacks can be prolonged, with attackers maintaining persistence in the network for a longer period of time.

5. The Internet of Things (IoT) and new attack vectors:

The proliferation of IoT devices has brought new challenges to cybersecurity. As everyday objects became connected to the Internet, they became potential targets for cyberattacks. Weak security measures in IoT devices have allowed attackers to exploit vulnerabilities, leading to incidents such as distributed denial of service (DDoS) attacks powered by compromised IoT botnets.

6. Ransomware and cyber extortion:
Ransomware attacks have increased in recent years, posing a serious threat to organizations of all sizes. Cybercriminals encrypt valuable data and demand a ransom for its release. The evolution of ransomware tactics includes not only file encryption but also the exfiltration of sensitive information, adding a layer of extortion to the attack.

7. Machine Learning and AI in Cyber Threats:
As defenders have adopted more advanced cybersecurity solutions, attackers have also taken advantage of cutting-edge technologies. Machine learning and artificial intelligence (AI) are now being used in cyber threats to improve evasion tactics,

automate attacks and adapt to changing defense strategies. This game of cat and mouse between attackers and defenders has reached new heights of sophistication.

8. Importance of cyber security solutions:
The evolution of cyber threats underscores the essential role of robust cyber security solutions. Traditional antivirus software has evolved into comprehensive cybersecurity suites that include features such as firewalls, intrusion detection systems, and behavioral analytics. Endpoint protection, network security, and identity management are critical components of defense against various cyber threats.

9. Threat intelligence and information sharing:
In response to the dynamic nature of cyber threats, the cybersecurity community emphasizes the importance of threat intelligence and information sharing. Collaborative efforts between security professionals, government agencies, and private organizations help identify emerging threats and

vulnerabilities, enabling a proactive response to potential cyber attacks.

10. Cyber hygiene and user awareness:
While technological solutions play a vital role, the human factor remains a significant element of cyber security. Educating users about cyber hygiene, promoting strong password practices, and raising awareness of social engineering tactics are essential components of a holistic cybersecurity strategy. Users are often the first line of defense against phishing and other socially engineered attacks.

The evolution of cyber threats has been marked by a continuous cycle of innovation and adaptation. As technology advances, so do the capabilities of cybercriminals. The landscape of cyber security solutions has evolved to meet these challenges and includes advanced technologies and collaborative approaches. Faced with an ever-changing threat landscape, a proactive and multifaceted cybersecurity strategy is essential to protect individuals, businesses and nations from the pervasive and evolving nature of cyber threats.

1.2 Importance of Cybersecurity in the Digital Age

In the ever-evolving environment of the digital age, the importance of cyber security cannot be overstated. As our world becomes increasingly interconnected through a vast network of technologies, the need for robust cybersecurity solutions has become paramount. From personal privacy to national security, the ramifications of cyber threats are far-reaching, making it essential to understand the importance of cyber security and the evolving solutions to protect us in this dynamic environment.

The Digital Age: The Double-Edged Sword

The digital age ushered in an era of unprecedented connectivity and technological advancement. With the proliferation of smart devices, cloud computing, and the Internet of Things (IoT), our lives have become more convenient, efficient, and connected than ever before. However, this interconnectedness has also exposed us to a myriad of cyber threats that pose significant risks to individuals, businesses and even nations.

Cyber Threat Landscape: Growing Concerns:

The cyber threat landscape is constantly evolving and cybercriminals are using increasingly sophisticated tactics to exploit vulnerabilities in our digital systems. From ransomware attacks that cripple businesses to identity theft that threatens personal privacy, the scope and impact of cyber threats are diverse and ever-expanding. Nation states are also active players in the cyber realm, engaging in cyber espionage, attacks on critical infrastructure, and even cyber warfare.

The Importance of Cyber Security: Protecting Individuals and Organizations:

At the core of the importance of cybersecurity is protecting individuals and organizations from the myriad threats that lurk in the digital realm. For individuals, cybersecurity protects personal data, financial information, and even physical well-being. In an age where online banking, social media and smart homes are the norm, compromising personal data can have serious consequences.

For businesses, the stakes are even higher. Cyber attacks can result in significant financial losses, reputational damage and legal consequences. The theft of sensitive business data, intellectual property or customer information can be catastrophic. Additionally, with supply chains becoming increasingly interconnected and dependent on digital infrastructure, a cyber attack on one entity can have cascading effects across the entire ecosystem.

On a national scale, cyber security is a key part of a country's defense and security strategy. State-sponsored cyber attacks can target critical infrastructure such as power grids, communications networks, and financial systems, posing a direct threat to national security. As cyber warfare becomes an integral part of modern conflict, states must invest in robust cyber security measures to protect their interests in the digital domain.

Cyber Security Solutions: A Multi-Pronged Approach:

Addressing the challenges posed by the complex cyber threat landscape requires a multifaceted approach to cybersecurity. Effective cyber security solutions include a range of technologies, policies and practices aimed at preventing, detecting and mitigating cyber threats.

1. Endpoint Security:

Protecting individual devices such as computers, smartphones and tablets is a fundamental aspect of cyber security. Endpoint security solutions include antivirus software, firewalls, and intrusion detection systems that protect devices from malicious software and unauthorized access.

2. Network Security:

Securing the networks that connect devices and systems is critical to preventing unauthorized access and data breaches. Firewalls, secure Wi-Fi protocols, and virtual private networks (VPNs) are key components of network security.

3. Identity and Access Management (IAM):

Controlling access to systems and data is essential to prevent unauthorized users from exploiting vulnerabilities. IAM solutions manage user identities, authentication and authorization and ensure that only authorized people have access to sensitive information.

4. Data Encryption: Encryption of sensitive data helps protect it from unauthorized access even if a breach occurs. Strong encryption algorithms ensure that even if data is captured, it remains unreadable without the appropriate decryption key.

5. Incident Response and Recovery:
Despite best efforts, no system is completely immune to cyber threats. Incident response and recovery plans are critical to minimizing the impact of a cyber attack, restoring systems to normal operations, and learning from the incident to increase future resilience.

6. Security Awareness Training:
Human error remains a significant factor in cyber security incidents. Educating individuals about the

risks of phishing, social engineering, and other common tactics allows them to make informed decisions and contribute to a culture of cybersecurity.

7. Collaboration and Information Sharing:
Cyber threats are not limited by borders and cooperation between organizations, industries and nations is key. Sharing information about emerging threats, vulnerabilities and best practices improves the collective defense against cyber adversaries.

The Future of Cyber Security: Challenges and Opportunities:
As technology advances, cybersecurity challenges are expected to evolve as well. The rise of artificial intelligence (AI) and machine learning (ML) brings both new opportunities for cybersecurity solutions and challenges posed by the potential misuse of these technologies by cybercriminals. If quantum computing were to be realized, it could render existing encryption methods obsolete, necessitating the development of quantum-resistant encryption.

Additionally, as our world becomes more connected with the advent of 5G technology and the proliferation of IoT devices, the attack surface for cyber threats is expanding. The proliferation of smart cities, autonomous vehicles, and critical infrastructure managed by connected systems underscores the urgency of addressing cybersecurity challenges in innovative ways.

Despite these challenges, the future of cybersecurity is also promising. Advances in AI and ML can be used to improve threat detection and response capabilities. Known for its decentralized, tamper-proof nature, blockchain technology shows potential for securing critical systems and transactions. As the cybersecurity landscape evolves, collaboration between governments, industries, and cybersecurity professionals will be essential to stay ahead of emerging threats.

The importance of cyber security in the digital age cannot be overstated. This is not just a technological problem, but a fundamental aspect of protecting our way of life in a connected world. Cybersecurity responsibilities range from individuals securing their personal devices to businesses protecting sensitive data and governments defending national interests. An investment in cyber security is an investment in the resilience and security of our digital society. As we navigate the complexity of the digital landscape, a shared commitment to cybersecurity, backed by robust solutions and proactive thinking, is essential to ensuring a safer and more secure future for individuals, businesses and nations.

Chapter 2. Common Cybersecurity Threats

In an era dominated by technology, the increasing dependence on digital platforms exposes individuals and organizations to a host of cyber security threats. From malware to sophisticated hacking techniques, these threats pose significant risks to the confidentiality, integrity and availability of sensitive information. Understanding these common cybersecurity threats and implementing robust solutions is paramount to protecting digital assets and maintaining a secure online environment.

1. Malware Attacks: A Persistent Threat:
Malicious software, or malware, remains one of the most pervasive cybersecurity threats. From viruses and worms to Trojans and ransomware, malware takes many forms, penetrating systems, compromising data and disrupting operations.

Users often encounter malware through phishing emails, insecure downloads or compromised websites.

Solution:

The use of comprehensive anti-virus and anti-malware solutions is essential. Regularly updating these programs, performing system checks, and educating users about safe online practices can significantly reduce the risk of malware attacks.

2. Phishing: Deceptive tactics for data leakage:

Phishing attacks involve fraudulent emails, messages, or websites designed to trick individuals into revealing sensitive information, such as login credentials or financial information. Cybercriminals often impersonate trusted entities to exploit human vulnerabilities.

Solution:

User education is key to fighting phishing. Organizations should conduct regular awareness training to help employees recognize phishing attempts. Additionally, implementing email filtering and multi-factor authentication (MFA) tools adds layers of defense against unauthorized access.

3. Ransomware: Holding Data Hostage:
Ransomware attacks have soared in recent years, with cybercriminals encrypting data and demanding payment for its release. These attacks can cripple businesses, disrupt critical services, and cause significant financial losses.

Solution:
Backing up your data regularly is critical to mitigating the impact of ransomware. Utilizing network segmentation, software updates, and investing in advanced threat detection systems increase overall resilience against ransomware attacks.

4. Insider Threats: A Trustworthy Risk:
Internal threats come from within the organization, either intentionally or unintentionally. Employees or suppliers can compromise sensitive information,

either maliciously or negligently, posing a significant cybersecurity challenge.

Solution:
Implementing strict access controls, monitoring user activity, and conducting regular security audits can help detect and prevent insider threats. Creating a culture of cybersecurity awareness and encouraging ethical behavior among employees are essential components of mitigating this risk.

5. DDoS Attacks: Overwhelming Online Resources:
DDoS (Distributed Denial of Service) attacks aim to overwhelm a system, network or website with a flood of traffic and make it inaccessible to legitimate users. This can lead to service interruptions and financial losses.

Solution:
Utilizing DDoS mitigation services, implementing firewalls, and configuring network settings to filter out malicious traffic are effective countermeasures against DDoS attacks. Regularly testing the

resilience of the system through simulated attacks can also identify weak points.

6. Weak Passwords: Gateway to Unauthorized Access:

Passwords serve as the primary line of defense, and weak or easy-to-guess passwords create vulnerabilities that cybercriminals can exploit. Password reuse and lack of regular updates exacerbate this risk.

Solution:

Enforcing strong password policies, supporting regular password changes, and implementing multi-factor authentication greatly increase security. Education in creating and managing secure passwords is key to user compliance.

7. Internet of Things (IoT) Vulnerabilities: Expanding Attack Surfaces:

The proliferation of IoT devices presents new avenues for cyber threats. Insecurely configured smart devices can be exploited to gain unauthorized access to networks, leading to data breaches and privacy concerns.

Solution:
Securing IoT devices through firmware updates, changing default credentials, and segmenting IoT networks from critical systems is imperative. Regular security assessments of IoT devices help identify and address vulnerabilities.

8. Zero-Day Exploits: Unseen Threats:
Zero-day exploits target vulnerabilities in software that are unknown to the vendor, making them particularly difficult to defend against. Cybercriminals exploit these vulnerabilities before developers can release patches.

Solution:
Keeping your software up-to-date with the latest patches is critical to reducing your exposure to zero-day exploits. The use of intrusion detection systems and the use of threat intelligence can help identify potential threats before they are widely exploited.

A Holistic Approach to Cyber Security.

As cyber threats are constantly evolving, a proactive and holistic approach to cyber security is essential. Combining technology solutions with user education, regular audits and a culture of security awareness creates a resilient defense against the ever-growing cyber threat landscape. By understanding common cybersecurity threats and implementing effective solutions, individuals and organizations can navigate the digital realm with confidence and protect their valuable assets from malicious actors.

2.1 Malware Attacks (Viruses, Worms, Trojans)

In an era dominated by technology, the constant threat of malware attacks looms over our interconnected digital environment. Commonly referred to as malware, malicious software comes in many forms, each with its own modus operandi and potential to wreak havoc. Viruses, worms and trojans are among the most widespread and insidious types of malware that pose significant challenges to the security of our digital assets. This contextual survey dives into the nature of these threats and examines the evolving landscape of cybersecurity solutions aimed at combating them.

Understanding the Enemy: Viruses, Worms and Trojans

Viruses: Like their biological namesakes, computer viruses are infectious entities that replicate by attaching to legitimate programs or files. Once a user runs an infected program, the virus becomes active and can spread throughout the system, often damaging or destroying data. Viruses can be transmitted through e-mail attachments, installation of infected software or compromised websites.

Worms: Worms, on the other hand, are self-replicating malware that do not require a host program to spread. They use vulnerabilities in network protocols to spread rapidly from one computer to another. Worms can consume network bandwidth, degrade system performance, and sometimes carry payloads that are harmful to the infected system.

Trojan Horses: Trojan horses, named after the legendary wooden horse, masquerade as legitimate software but contain malicious code. Unlike viruses and worms, Trojan horses do not replicate themselves. Instead, they rely on social engineering to get users to install them. Once activated, Trojans can facilitate unauthorized access, data theft, or the installation of additional malware.

Cybersecurity Challenge: The Constant Battle

In an ever-evolving cybersecurity landscape, staying ahead of malware threats requires a multi-pronged approach. Traditional antivirus solutions, once the mainstay of defense, are now just one component of a broader strategy. The following sections describe key cybersecurity measures and solutions that together form a formidable defense against malware attacks.

1. Antivirus Software: The First Line of Defense

Antivirus software remains an essential tool in the fight against malware. These programs detect, quarantine, and eliminate known viruses, worms, and Trojans. Signature-based detection, heuristic analysis, and behavioral monitoring are common techniques used by antivirus solutions to identify and neutralize malicious code. Regular updates to virus definitions ensure that the software stays up-to-date with the latest threats.

2. Endpoint protection: Device and network protection

Endpoint protection goes beyond traditional antivirus measures to include a wider range of security features. It includes firewalls, intrusion detection systems and behavioral analysis tools. By securing individual devices and network endpoints, this approach reduces the risk of malware infiltrating an organization's infrastructure.

3. Patch Management: Vulnerability Closures

Many malware attacks exploit vulnerabilities in software or operating systems. Regular software updates and patches are essential to address these security vulnerabilities. Cybersecurity professionals must take a proactive approach to patch management and ensure all systems are up-to-date and protected against known vulnerabilities.

4. User Education: Building a Human Firewall
Human error remains a significant factor in successful malware attacks. Educating users about the risks associated with phishing emails, suspicious attachments and unverified downloads is essential. Building an alert and informed user base acts as a human firewall to prevent the inadvertent installation of malware.

5. Network Security: Perimeter Fortification
A robust network security infrastructure acts as a critical barrier against malware attacks. Firewalls, intrusion prevention systems, and secure network configurations help prevent unauthorized access and block malicious traffic. Regular network monitoring and analysis is essential to identify unusual patterns that may indicate a malware intrusion.

6. Advanced Threat Detection: Uncover Stealth Malware

As malware becomes more sophisticated, advanced threat detection technologies have emerged to identify and neutralize previously unknown threats. Machine learning, artificial intelligence and behavioral analytics play a key role in recognizing patterns indicating malware activity, even as traditional signature-based methods lag behind.

7. Incident Response and Recovery: Damage Minimization

No cybersecurity defense is foolproof, so incident response and recovery capabilities are indispensable. Organizations must have well-defined protocols for detecting, isolating and mitigating the impact of a malware incident. Regular testing of these response plans ensures readiness in the face of a real threat.

A Holistic Approach to Cyber Security

In the ongoing fight against malware attacks, cybersecurity is not a one-size-fits-all solution. A holistic approach that combines traditional antivirus measures with advanced threat detection, user education and robust network security is essential. As technology evolves, so must our defense strategies against the ever-adapting malware threat landscape. By adopting a multi-layered defense and fostering a culture of cybersecurity awareness, we can collectively protect our digital realm from the ever-present and evolving threats posed by viruses, worms and Trojan horses.

2.2 Phishing and Social Engineering

In the rapidly evolving cybersecurity landscape, the threats posed by phishing and social engineering are becoming more significant and sophisticated. As technology advances, so do the tactics used by malicious actors seeking to exploit vulnerabilities in human behavior. This contextual content delves into the complex world of phishing and social engineering, exploring their intricacies and implications for cybersecurity, while shedding light on preventative measures and solutions to mitigate these risks.

Phishing: The Scam;

Phishing is a cyberattack technique that relies on deception to trick individuals into revealing sensitive information such as usernames, passwords, or financial information. Typically delivered via email, instant messaging or malicious websites, phishing attacks often masquerade as trustworthy entities and create a false sense of legitimacy. Attackers use psychological tactics to manipulate the recipient into taking actions that benefit the malicious actor.

Social Engineering: Harnessing Human Psychology:

Social engineering is a broader concept encompassing various manipulative techniques that use human psychology to gain unauthorized access, information or resources. It goes beyond the digital realm, often involving face-to-face interactions or phone calls. An attacker manipulates individuals into divulging confidential information or taking actions that may compromise security.

Phishing can be viewed as a subset of social engineering, focusing specifically on deceptive digital communications.

The evolving threat landscape

Tactical Sophistication:
As cyber security measures become more robust, cybercriminals are constantly refining their tactics. Phishing attacks are no longer limited to poorly crafted emails with obvious red flags. Instead, attackers use advanced techniques such as spear phishing, where messages are tailored to target specific individuals or organizations. This personalized approach increases the likelihood of success because it benefits from the familiarity and trust between the attacker and the target.

Using current events:
Phishers often take advantage of current events, use global crises or popular trends to increase the effectiveness of their attacks. For example, during the COVID-19 pandemic, cybercriminals launched phishing campaigns posing as healthcare

organizations, using fear and uncertainty to trick individuals into clicking on malicious links or providing sensitive information.

Implications for cyber security

Data Breach and Financial Losses:
The consequences of falling victim to phishing and social engineering attacks can be severe. Data breaches, resulting from the compromise of credentials or sensitive information, expose individuals and organizations to many risks. Financial losses, identity theft, and reputational damage are common outcomes, underscoring the critical importance of robust cybersecurity measures.

Threatened networks and systems:
In addition to individual targets, successful phishing and social engineering attacks can compromise entire networks and systems. Once an attacker gains access, they can escalate privileges, install malware, or initiate other attacks, which can lead to significant disruption to operations and services.

Education and Awareness:
One of the fundamental pillars in the fight against phishing and social engineering is education. Individuals must be aware of attacker tactics and equipped with the knowledge to identify and report suspicious activity. Regular cyber security training, simulated phishing exercises and awareness campaigns contribute to building an alert and informed user base.

Advanced email security measures:
As email remains the primary vector for phishing attacks, organizations should invest in advanced email security solutions. These can include spam filters, sender verification protocols, and threat integration to detect and block malicious emails before they reach users' inboxes.

Multi-Factor Authentication (MFA):
Implementing multi-factor authentication adds another layer of security by requiring users to verify

their identity in multiple ways. Even if attackers get the credentials, MFA acts as a deterrent because they would still need a second form of authentication.

Regular security audits and updates:
Frequent security audits and updates are essential to identify and patch vulnerabilities. Organizations should regularly assess their systems, networks and applications to ensure they are protected against emerging threats. Maintaining up-to-date software and security protocols is an essential part of a robust cybersecurity strategy.

Incident Response Plans:
Having a well-defined incident response plan is critical to minimizing the impact of a successful phishing or social engineering attack. This plan should outline the steps to be taken in the event of a security incident, including communication strategies, containment measures, and post-incident analysis.
In an ever-expanding digital environment, combating phishing and social engineering is a

constant challenge. As technology advances, so do the tactics of malicious actors. However, by understanding the complexity of these threats and implementing comprehensive cybersecurity solutions, individuals and organizations can strengthen their defenses and navigate the digital realm with greater resilience. Education, advanced security measures and proactive strategies are key to mitigating the risks posed by phishing and social engineering, ensuring a safer and more secure cyberspace for all.

2.3 Denial of Service (DoS) and Distributed Denial of Service (DDoS)

In the ever-evolving cybersecurity landscape, Denial of Service (DoS) and Distributed Denial of Service (DDoS) attacks pose significant threats to organizations, individuals, and even nations. These malicious activities aim to disrupt the availability of online services, cause serious financial losses, damage reputations and compromise the integrity of critical systems. This article examines the nuances of DoS and DDoS attacks, their potential impacts, and the comprehensive cybersecurity solutions available to thwart these threats.

Understanding DoS and DDoS Attacks:

Denial of Service (DoS) attacks occur when a malicious actor floods a targeted system, network, or service, making it inaccessible to legitimate users. This is achieved by flooding the target with a large volume of traffic, exhausting its resources and bandwidth. On the other hand, DDoS (Distributed Denial of Service) attacks involve multiple compromised devices, forming a botnet that collectively overwhelms the target, making it difficult to mitigate.

Potential impacts of DoS and DDoS attacks:

1. Financial Losses: Organizations can suffer significant financial losses due to downtime, lost productivity and damage to their online reputation. E-commerce platforms, financial institutions and service providers are particularly vulnerable.

2. Reputation Damage: Customers and clients may lose confidence in an organization that experiences frequent outages or failures. This can have long-term consequences that affect customer loyalty and market position.

3. Operation Disruption: Critical infrastructure such as power grids, healthcare systems and emergency services can face operational disruptions during a DoS or DDoS attack, putting lives at risk.

4. Intellectual Property Theft: In some cases, attackers can exploit the chaos caused by these attacks to infiltrate and steal sensitive information, intellectual property, or personal data.

A comprehensive cyber security solution:

1. Traffic Filtering and Monitoring:
    - Use robust traffic filtering mechanisms to distinguish between legitimate and malicious traffic.
    - Implement continuous monitoring to detect unusual patterns and anomalies in network behavior.

2. Redundancy and load balancing:

- Distribute network traffic across multiple servers using load balancing techniques to ensure no single point of failure.

- Create redundant systems and data centers to maintain service availability during an attack.

3. Intrusion Prevention Systems (IPS):

- Deploy IPS to detect and block malicious activity in real time.

- Use anomaly-based detection to identify deviations from normal network behavior.

4. Content Delivery Networks (CDNs):

- Leverage CDNs to geographically distribute content and reduce the impact of DDoS attacks by spreading the load across multiple servers.

- Leverage CDN caching to mitigate the impact on the origin server during an attack.

5. Rate Limiting and Traffic Shaping:

- Implement rate limiting to control the amount of incoming traffic to prevent network congestion.

- Use traffic shaping to prioritize and allocate bandwidth to critical services during an attack.

6. Web Application Gateways (WAFs):
   - Use a WAF to filter and monitor HTTP traffic between a web application and the Internet.
   - Configure WAF rules to block malicious requests and protect against application layer attacks.

7. Incident Response Planning:
   - Create and regularly update an incident response plan for effective mitigation and recovery from DoS and DDoS attacks.
   - Conduct regular drills to ensure the readiness and effectiveness of response teams.

8. Collaboration and Information Sharing:
   - Join industry Information Sharing and Analysis Centers (ISACs) to exchange threat information and best practices.
   - Cooperate with other organizations to jointly strengthen cyber security.

Denial of Service and Distributed Denial of Service attacks are constantly evolving, making them persistent threats in the digital realm. A comprehensive cybersecurity strategy that combines proactive measures, advanced detection mechanisms, and rapid response capabilities is critical to mitigating the impact of these attacks. As organizations adapt to the changing threat landscape, implementing multifaceted cybersecurity solutions is becoming imperative to protect critical assets, maintain service availability, and maintain stakeholder trust in an increasingly connected world.

2.4 Insider Threats

In the ever-evolving cybersecurity landscape, one of the most persistent and complex challenges facing organizations is the insider threat. Insider threats refer to the risks associated with individuals within an organization who have the potential to abuse their access and privileges to compromise the confidentiality, integrity, or availability of sensitive information. These individuals may be employees, suppliers, or business partners, making it essential for organizations to adopt a comprehensive cybersecurity solution to mitigate the risks associated with insider threats.

Understanding Insider Threats:

Insider threats can take many forms, from inadvertent actions to malicious intent. Employees may unwittingly compromise security by falling victim to phishing attacks, while others may intentionally engage in activities such as data theft, espionage, or unauthorized access. The motivation behind insider threats can include financial gain, personal grievances, or even ideological reasons. Identifying and addressing these threats requires a nuanced approach that combines technology solutions, policy frameworks and employee awareness.

Technological solutions:

1. User Behavior Analysis (UBA):

Implementing UBA tools allows organizations to monitor and analyze user activities and identify deviations from normal behavior. These tools use machine learning algorithms to detect anomalies and potential insider threats and provide organizations with early alerts to take preventative action.

2. Data Loss Prevention (DLP) systems:

DLP systems are key to preventing unauthorized access, use or transfer of sensitive data. By classifying and monitoring data, organizations can set policies to block or restrict the movement of critical information, reducing the risk of valuable assets being compromised from the inside.

3. Identity and Access Management (IAM):

IAM systems help organizations manage user access rights and permissions. By enforcing the principle of least privilege, IAM solutions ensure that individuals have the necessary access to perform their roles without unnecessary privileges that could be misused for malicious purposes.

Policy frameworks:

1. Clear Acceptable Use Policy:

Establishing and communicating clear acceptable use policies helps establish employee expectations for the appropriate use of organizational resources. These policies should outline the consequences of violating security protocols and emphasize the importance of protecting sensitive information.

2. Incident Response Plans:

Developing comprehensive incident response plans is essential for organizations to effectively address insider threats when they occur. A well-defined plan outlines the steps to take in the event of a security incident, helping to minimize the impact and prevent further damage.

3. Continuous monitoring and auditing:

Regular monitoring and auditing of user activities can help identify potential insider threats. By maintaining a vigilant posture, organizations can quickly detect and respond to suspicious behavior and mitigate the risks associated with insider threats.

Employee Awareness:

1. Training and Education:

Investing in employee cybersecurity training is paramount. Educating employees about the different forms of insider threats, the importance of safe practices, and the consequences of careless behavior can empower them to take an active role in maintaining a safe environment.

2. Cultivating a Security Culture:

Fostering a culture of security within the organization encourages employees to make cybersecurity a priority. This includes creating a sense of shared responsibility for protecting sensitive information and reporting any suspicious activity immediately.

Effectively addressing insider cybersecurity threats requires a multifaceted approach that combines technology solutions, policy frameworks, and employee awareness. Organizations must recognize the dynamic nature of insider threats and constantly adapt their strategies to stay ahead of potential risks. By integrating advanced technologies, implementing robust policies and fostering a security-focused culture, organizations can significantly reduce the likelihood and impact of insider threats and strengthen their cybersecurity posture in an increasingly connected digital environment.

2.5 Advanced Persistent Threats (APTs)

Advanced Persistent Threats (APTs) represent a significant and evolving cybersecurity challenge. These sophisticated and targeted attacks are characterized by persistence, stealth and often extended periods of time during which attackers remain undetected on the network. To effectively counter the threats posed by APTs, cybersecurity solutions must take a multifaceted approach that combines advanced technology, threat intelligence, and proactive strategies.

Understanding Advanced Persistent Threats (APT): APTs are not your typical cyber attacks. Unlike opportunistic and short-term attacks, APTs are organized by well-funded and highly skilled threat actors with specific goals, such as espionage, data theft, or disruption of critical infrastructure. These attackers are patient, often lurking in the system for long periods of time, carefully studying the target environment, and discreetly exploiting vulnerabilities.

1. Stealth and Persistence:

APTs use a variety of sophisticated techniques to avoid detection. They can use their own malware, use encryption, and blend in with normal network traffic to remain stealthy. The persistent nature of APTs allows attackers to adapt their tactics over time, making it difficult to defend against with traditional security measures.

Cyber security solution for APT

Addressing APT requires a comprehensive and adaptive cybersecurity strategy. Below are the key components of an effective solution:

1. Advanced Threat Detection:

Leveraging advanced threat detection mechanisms is critical to identifying APTs early in their lifecycle. Machine learning algorithms and behavioral analytics play a key role in recognizing patterns indicative of malicious activity. This proactive approach allows organizations to detect anomalies and potential threats before significant damage occurs.

2. Endpoint Security:

Securing individual endpoints is critical because APTs often target specific devices to gain access to a network. Endpoint protection solutions should include robust antivirus software, endpoint detection and response (EDR) capabilities, and continuous monitoring to identify and respond to suspicious activity on devices.

3. Network monitoring and segmentation:

Implementing continuous network monitoring helps in detecting unusual patterns or activities within the network. Additionally, network segmentation ensures that even if one segment is compromised, the lateral movement of attackers is limited, limiting the potential damage they can cause.

4. Threat Information Sharing:

Collaboration is key in the fight against APTs. Sharing threat information with industry peers and participating in information sharing initiatives increases the collective ability to identify and thwart APTs. Access to timely and relevant threat intelligence enables organizations to stay ahead of emerging threats and strengthen their defenses accordingly.

5. Incident Response Planning:

Preparing for the inevitability of a security incident is essential. A well-defined incident response plan ensures that organizations can respond quickly and effectively to APTs when they are detected. This includes isolating affected systems, investigating the extent of the compromise, and immediately implementing corrective actions.

6. User Training and Awareness:

APTs often exploit human vulnerabilities through techniques such as phishing. Educating users about cybersecurity best practices, raising awareness of potential threats, and conducting regular training can significantly reduce the likelihood of them falling victim to APTs.

7. Regular security audits and vulnerability management:

Conducting regular security audits and proactively managing vulnerabilities are essential aspects of APT defense. Early identification and patching of vulnerabilities prevents attackers from exploiting known weaknesses in the system.

8. Next generation firewalls and intrusion prevention systems:

Deploying advanced firewalls and intrusion prevention systems adds another layer of defense against APTs. These systems use advanced techniques such as deep packet inspection and threat intelligence integration to block malicious traffic and prevent unauthorized access.

9. Data encryption and access control:

Implementing strong data encryption measures and strict access controls ensures that even if an APT manages to infiltrate a network, the potential damage is limited. Encrypting sensitive information and restricting access to authorized persons minimizes the impact of a successful breach.

In the ever-evolving cybersecurity landscape, combating advanced persistent threats requires constant vigilance and a proactive attitude. To defend against these sophisticated adversaries, organizations must invest in a combination of cutting-edge technology, threat intelligence sharing, and robust cybersecurity practices. By adopting a multi-layered approach that includes detection, prevention and response, businesses can significantly increase their resilience to APTs and protect their critical assets from exploitation. As APTs continue to evolve, so must our cybersecurity solutions to ensure they stay one step ahead of the persistent and advanced threats that threaten the digital landscape.

Chapter 3. Cybersecurity Solutions and Technologies

In an era dominated by digital interactions and technological advancements, the significance of cybersecurity has never been more pronounced. As organizations and individuals increasingly rely on digital platforms and networks for communication, transactions, and data storage, the need for robust cybersecurity solutions and technologies becomes paramount. This contextual content explores the evolution of cybersecurity solutions, the current landscape of cybersecurity technologies, and the challenges that persist in securing the digital realm.

Cybersecurity is a multidimensional field encompassing a range of strategies, technologies, and practices aimed at protecting computers, networks, and data from unauthorized access, attacks, and damage. The rapid proliferation of digital systems has brought about an intricate web of vulnerabilities, making cybersecurity an integral component of the modern technological landscape.

I. Evolution of Cybersecurity Solutions:

The evolution of cybersecurity solutions can be traced back to the early days of computing when security measures primarily focused on physical access control. Over time, as networks expanded and interconnected, the emphasis shifted towards developing encryption techniques and access controls at the software level. The 2000s witnessed a surge in cybersecurity awareness, prompted by high-profile cyber attacks, leading to the development of more sophisticated solutions.

1. Antivirus Software and Firewalls:

In the early 2000s, antivirus software and firewalls emerged as foundational cybersecurity tools. Antivirus programs were designed to detect and remove malicious software, while firewalls acted as barriers between internal networks and the untrusted external environment. These solutions were effective in mitigating a range of threats but struggled to keep pace with the evolving tactics of cybercriminals.

2. Intrusion Detection and Prevention Systems

As cyber threats became more sophisticated, intrusion detection and prevention systems gained prominence. These technologies aimed to identify and respond to potential threats in real-time, providing a proactive defense against various attack vectors. The integration of machine learning and artificial intelligence further enhanced the capabilities of these systems, enabling them to adapt to new threats dynamically.

3. Endpoint Security:

The rise of remote work and the proliferation of mobile devices led to the development of endpoint security solutions. Endpoint protection involves securing individual devices like computers, smartphones, and tablets from cyber threats. This approach became crucial as traditional network boundaries blurred, and cybercriminals sought new avenues for exploitation.

II. Current Landscape of Cybersecurity Technologies:

In the contemporary digital landscape, cybersecurity solutions have evolved into a diverse ecosystem of technologies, each serving a specific purpose in safeguarding against cyber threats.

1. Next-Generation Firewalls:

Next-generation firewalls integrate traditional firewall capabilities with advanced functionalities such as intrusion prevention, application awareness, and deep packet inspection. These solutions provide more granular control over network traffic and enhance the ability to detect and prevent sophisticated cyber attacks.

2. Advanced Persistent Threat (APT) Protection:

Advanced Persistent Threats represent a category of sophisticated, targeted cyber attacks that often go undetected by traditional security measures. APT protection solutions leverage advanced analytics and threat intelligence to identify and neutralize these prolonged and stealthy attacks, offering a proactive defense against persistent adversaries.

3. Security Information and Event Management (SIEM):

SIEM solutions aggregate and analyze log data from various sources across an organization's IT infrastructure. By correlating information and detecting patterns indicative of security incidents, SIEM tools enable organizations to respond swiftly to potential threats. The integration of machine learning enhances SIEM capabilities, allowing for more accurate threat detection.

4. Cloud Security:

With the widespread adoption of cloud computing, securing data and applications hosted in the cloud has become a critical aspect of cybersecurity. Cloud security solutions encompass identity and access management, data encryption, and threat detection mechanisms tailored for cloud environments, ensuring the protection of sensitive information in the digital realm.

III. Emerging Technologies in Cybersecurity:

As cyber threats continue to evolve, the cybersecurity landscape is shaped by emerging technologies that hold the promise of enhanced protection and resilience.

1. Artificial Intelligence and Machine Learning:

Artificial intelligence (AI) and machine learning (ML) have become integral to cybersecurity by enabling systems to learn and adapt to new threats autonomously. AI-driven solutions can analyze vast datasets, identify patterns, and detect anomalies indicative of cyber attacks, providing a more proactive and responsive defense.

2. Zero Trust Architecture:

Zero Trust Architecture is a paradigm shift in cybersecurity that assumes no trust, even among entities within the network. This approach requires continuous verification of user identity and device security before granting access to resources. Zero Trust minimizes the attack surface and limits the potential impact of security breaches.

3. Quantum-Safe Cryptography:

The advent of quantum computing poses a potential threat to traditional cryptographic algorithms. Quantum-safe cryptography aims to develop encryption methods that remain secure even in the face of quantum computers, ensuring the long-term resilience of cybersecurity measures.

IV. Challenges in Cybersecurity:

Despite the advancements in cybersecurity solutions and technologies, challenges persist in the ongoing battle against cyber threats.

1. Cybersecurity Skills Gap:

The demand for skilled cybersecurity professionals far exceeds the available talent pool, leading to a significant skills gap. Addressing this challenge requires concerted efforts in education, training, and workforce development to cultivate a skilled and diverse cybersecurity workforce.

2. Rapidly Evolving Threat Landscape:

Cyber threats are dynamic and ever-evolving, making it challenging for cybersecurity solutions to keep pace. Continuous research and development, threat intelligence sharing, and collaboration among cybersecurity professionals are essential to staying ahead of emerging threats.

3. Compliance and Regulatory Complexity:
The complexity of cybersecurity regulations and compliance requirements varies across industries and jurisdictions. Organizations must navigate a complex landscape of standards and regulations, often requiring substantial resources to ensure compliance while maintaining effective security measures.

V. Future Directions in Cybersecurity:
Looking ahead, the future of cybersecurity will likely be shaped by ongoing technological advancements and evolving threat landscapes.

1. Integration of Quantum Computing:
While quantum computing poses a potential threat, it also offers opportunities for enhancing cybersecurity. Quantum-resistant algorithms and cryptographic methods will play a crucial role in

securing digital communication and data against quantum-enabled attacks.

2. Autonomous Security Systems:

The integration of AI and ML will continue to drive the development of autonomous security systems capable of identifying, responding to, and mitigating cyber threats in real-time. These systems will reduce reliance on manual intervention and enhance the speed and accuracy of threat detection.

3. Cybersecurity in the Internet of Things (IoT):

The proliferation of IoT devices introduces new challenges in terms of security vulnerabilities. Future cybersecurity solutions will need to address the unique risks associated with interconnected devices, ensuring the protection of both individual users and critical infrastructure.

Cybersecurity solutions and technologies play a pivotal role in safeguarding the digital realm against an ever-evolving array of cyber threats. The historical progression from antivirus software to advanced threat detection systems reflects the dynamic nature of the field. As emerging technologies like AI, Zero Trust Architecture, and quantum safe cryptography continue to shape the landscape, addressing challenges such as the skills gap and regulatory complexity becomes paramount. The future of cybersecurity promises continued innovation and adaptation to counter emerging threats, ensuring the resilience and security of the interconnected digital world.

3.1 Antivirus and Anti-malware Solutions

In an era dominated by digital advancements, the threat landscape for individuals and organizations has evolved dramatically. With increasing reliance on technology, the risk of becoming a victim of cyber threats has become a ubiquitous concern. In this digital age where information is a valuable asset, protection against malicious attacks is paramount. Antivirus and anti malware solutions play a key role in strengthening the defenses of individuals and organizations against the ever evolving cyber threat landscape.

Understanding the Cyber Threat Landscape:

Cyber threats come in many forms, from traditional viruses to sophisticated malware, ransomware and more. These threats exploit vulnerabilities in software, networks, and human behavior to compromise the confidentiality, integrity, and availability of data. As technology evolves, so do the methods used by cybercriminals, requiring a proactive and robust cybersecurity strategy.

Role of antivirus and antimalware solutions:

Antivirus and anti-malware solutions are essential components of cyber security strategies and act as the first line of defense against malicious software. These solutions are designed to detect, prevent, and remove malicious code that could compromise system security. They use a combination of signature-based detection, behavioral analysis and heuristics to identify and neutralize threats.

Signature based detection:

Traditional antivirus solutions rely on a database of known malware signatures. These signatures are unique characteristics or patterns associated with specific strains of malware. When a file or program is scanned, the antivirus software compares its signature with the signatures in its database. If a match is found, the software marks the file as malicious.

Behavior Analysis:

As cyber threats become more sophisticated, traditional signature-based detection alone may not be sufficient. Behavioral analysis involves monitoring the behavior of programs in real time. If a program exhibits suspicious or malicious behavior, it is flagged and blocked, even if its signature is not in the antivirus database.

Heuristics:

Heuristic analysis involves identifying new, previously unknown malware based on its behavior and characteristics. Instead of relying on predefined signatures, heuristics allow antivirus software to detect and block emerging threats that exhibit patterns of malicious activity.

Comprehensive protection beyond traditional antivirus:

While antivirus solutions provide a critical layer of protection, the evolving nature of cyber threats requires a more comprehensive approach. Anti-malware solutions complement traditional anti-virus measures by addressing a wider range of malicious software, including Trojans, spyware, adware and other potentially unwanted programs (PUPs).

Anti-Malware Capabilities:

Anti-malware solutions go beyond traditional viruses and often include features to detect and remove a wider range of threats. They are designed to identify and eliminate various types of malware that may not be covered by standard antivirus signatures.

Real-time Protection:

Both antivirus and anti-malware solutions offer real-time protection and actively monitor system activity to detect and block threats as they appear.

This proactive approach helps prevent infections before they can cause damage.

Regular Updates:
Antivirus and antimalware solutions require regular updates to remain effective against new and emerging threats. These updates include new malware signatures, heuristics, and behavioral analysis patterns that ensure security software stays up-to-date and capable of countering the latest threats.

Challenges and Limitations:
Despite their effectiveness, antivirus and antimalware solutions face challenges when it comes to keeping up with the dynamic threat landscape. Cybercriminals are constantly devising new techniques to evade detection, such as polymorphic malware, which changes its code to evade signature-based identification. Additionally, the rise of fileless malware, which operates in system memory without leaving traditional traces, is challenging conventional detection methods.

Integrated security solutions:

Many cybersecurity strategies now emphasize integration, recognizing the limitations of stand-alone antivirus and antimalware solutions. Integrated security solutions combine various tools and technologies, including firewalls, intrusion detection systems and endpoint security, to create a layered defense. This multifaceted approach increases an organization's overall cybersecurity resilience.

Endpoint Protection:

Endpoint protection solutions go beyond traditional antivirus programs by securing individual devices (endpoints) within a network. These solutions often include features such as application control, device control, and advanced threat protection to protect against a wide variety of threats.

Cloud security:

As businesses move to cloud environments, cloud security solutions are becoming an integral part of comprehensive cyber security. These solutions provide real-time threat intelligence, data loss prevention, and secure access control to protect data stored and processed in the cloud.

In the ever evolving cybersecurity landscape, antivirus and anti malware solutions remain essential components of defense. While traditional antivirus tools play a key role in identifying known threats, the inclusion of anti malware features and integration with other security measures is essential for comprehensive protection. Organizations and individuals must take a proactive stance, stay informed of emerging threats, and apply a layered security approach to mitigate the risks posed by an increasingly sophisticated and dynamic cyber threat landscape.

3.2 Firewalls and Intrusion Detection Systems (IDS)

In a dynamic cybersecurity environment where digital threats are constantly evolving, the roles of firewalls and intrusion detection systems (IDS) are paramount. These two components form a formidable line of defense and strengthen networks and systems against cyber threats. In this comprehensive survey, we delve into the intricacies of firewalls and IDS, examining their functions, importance, and how their symbiotic relationship contributes to a robust cybersecurity solution.

Firewalls: Fortifying the Digital Perimeter:
At the forefront of network security, firewalls act as digital watchdogs, monitoring and controlling incoming and outgoing network traffic. Similar to a physical barrier, firewalls create a perimeter defense by examining data packets and determining whether to allow or block them based on predefined security rules. This fundamental aspect of cyber security plays a key role in preventing unauthorized access and securing sensitive information.

Types of firewalls:
Firewalls come in a variety of forms, each tailored to specific needs and scenarios. Network layer firewalls operating at the network layer of the OSI model examine packet headers and make access decisions. Stateful inspection firewalls, on the other hand, monitor the state of active connections,

allowing for more sophisticated filtering. Proxy firewalls act as intermediaries between end users and the Internet and serve as a barrier between internal systems and external networks.

Firewall functionality:
Firewalls use a number of techniques to control and filter traffic. Packet filtering involves examining packet headers for source and destination addresses, ports, and protocols. Stateful inspection, as mentioned earlier, considers the context of active connections. Proxying involves acting as an intermediary for communication, preventing a direct link between internal and external systems. Together, these mechanisms contribute to a multi-layered defense and mitigate various cyber threats.

Intrusion Detection Systems (IDS): Vigilant Sentinels:
While firewalls form the initial line of defense, Intrusion Detection Systems (IDS) provide a second layer of protection by actively monitoring and analyzing network and system activity. Unlike

firewalls, which are primarily focused on access control, IDSs are designed to detect and respond to malicious activity that may have bypassed the initial barrier. This proactive approach is essential to identifying and thwarting sophisticated cyber threats.

Types of IDS:
IDS can generally be divided into two categories: Network-based IDS (NIDS) and Host-based IDS (HIDS). NIDS analyzes network traffic, identifying suspicious patterns or anomalies. HIDS, on the other hand, focuses on activities occurring on individual devices, monitoring system logs and file integrity. This dual approach provides end-to-end coverage and addresses both network-wide and device-specific threats.

Detection Techniques:
IDS uses various detection techniques to identify potential security incidents. Signature-based detection involves comparing observed activities against a database of known attack patterns or signatures. On the other hand, anomaly-based

detection identifies deviations from established baselines and recognizes abnormal behavior that may indicate a security breach. The combination of these techniques increases the ability of IDS to detect both known and unknown threats.

Symbiosis in Action: Firewall and IDS Integration:
While firewalls and IDS serve different purposes, their integration creates a synergistic defense mechanism. Firewalls create a secure perimeter, prevent unauthorized access and filter out potential threats. However, in the ever-evolving cyber threat landscape, some malicious activities may evade initial defenses.

This is where IDS comes in. By actively monitoring network traffic and system activities, an IDS can identify suspicious patterns or anomalies that may indicate a security breach. When integrated with firewalls, IDS can provide real-time feedback, enabling dynamic adjustments to security rules. For example, if an IDS detects a new type of attack, firewall rules can be instantly updated to block such threats, creating a responsive and adaptive security infrastructure.

Challenges and Considerations:

While firewalls and IDS are an integral part of cyber security, their effectiveness depends on several factors. Over-reliance on signature-based detection can leave an IDS vulnerable to unknown threats, highlighting the importance of incorporating anomaly-based detection and behavioral analysis. Additionally, false positives and negatives remain persistent problems. Finding the right balance between a robust security posture and minimizing disruption to legitimate activities requires ongoing fine-tuning and calibration. Regular updates to threat databases, security rules, and system configurations are essential to stay ahead of emerging threats.

Evolution in the Face of Emerging Threats:

As cyber threats become more sophisticated, the development of firewalls and IDS is paramount. Next-generation firewalls (NGFWs) integrate advanced features such as deep packet inspection, application layer filtering, and intrusion prevention systems to increase the depth and breadth of protection.

Similarly, IDS solutions are evolving to include machine learning and artificial intelligence algorithms. These enhancements allow IDS to adapt to evolving threats, learning from patterns and behaviors to increase detection accuracy. The integration of threat intelligence sources further strengthens these systems and provides real-time information on emerging threats and vulnerabilities.

A united front against cyber threats:

In an ever-expanding digital frontier where cyber threats lurk around every virtual corner, the synergy between firewalls and intrusion detection systems is indispensable. Firewalls create a strong perimeter defense, while IDS provides a vigilant second layer that actively monitors and responds to potential security incidents. The integration of these components creates a united front that strengthens the cyber landscape against myriad threats.

As organizations navigate the complex terrain of cybersecurity, a holistic approach that combines robust firewalls, adaptive IDS, and continuous monitoring is essential. By understanding the fine interplay between these components, cybersecurity professionals can build resilient defense strategies, protect digital assets, and ensure information integrity in a connected world.

3.3 Encryption Technologies

Encryption technologies play a key role in strengthening cybersecurity solutions and serve as an indispensable safeguard against unauthorized access and data breaches. In an age dominated by digital interactions, protecting sensitive information is paramount. This comprehensive survey delves into the importance of encryption in cybersecurity, its underlying principles, and its many-sided applications.

Cyber security is a complex landscape with threats evolving in sophistication and frequency. Encryption proves to be a formidable shield against these threats and works as an encryption technique to convert plain text into an unreadable format. Its application covers various aspects of cyber security, including data protection, secure communication and critical infrastructure security.

Principles of Encryption

At its core, encryption relies on robust mathematical algorithms that transform data into an unintelligible form, often referred to as ciphertext. This transformation requires a cryptographic key, a key element in the encryption and decryption process. The key acts as a digital lock and only the one with the correct key can unlock and decrypt the information.

Encryption uses two primary categories of algorithms: symmetric and asymmetric. Symmetric encryption involves the use of a single key for both encryption and decryption, while asymmetric encryption uses a pair of keys – a public key for encryption and a private key for decryption. The interplay between these keys forms the basis of secure communication channels.

Data Protection:

One of the fundamental applications of encryption in cyber security is data protection. Organizations collect vast amounts of sensitive information, from customer data to proprietary algorithms, so protecting this data becomes a must. Encryption ensures that even if unauthorized parties gain access to the data, the data remains indecipherable without the appropriate cryptographic key.

End-to-end encryption, often used in messaging apps and file-sharing services, ensures that only designated recipients can access the data being transferred. This is especially important in industries such as healthcare and finance, where the confidentiality of personal and financial information is non negotiable.

Secure Communication:

In the field of cyber security, secure communication channels are key. Encryption makes it easier to create these secure channels, thwarting eavesdropping attempts and man-in-the-middle attacks. Virtual Private Networks (VPNs) use encryption to create a secure tunnel through the Internet that protects sensitive data as it travels through the digital landscape.

Secure Sockets Layer (SSL) and its successor, Transport Layer Security (TLS), are protocols that use encryption to securely transmit data over the web. These protocols are an integral part of online transactions and ensure the confidentiality and integrity of information exchanged between users and websites.

Mitigating Insider Threats:
While external threats often grab the headlines, insider threats pose a significant risk to cybersecurity. Encryption serves as a strong deterrent against malicious insiders seeking unauthorized access to sensitive information. By encrypting data at rest, even if an employee or insider gains access to the storage infrastructure, the encrypted data remains unreadable without the corresponding decryption key.

Regulatory Compliance:
The regulatory landscape surrounding data privacy and security is constantly evolving. Encryption often serves as a cornerstone of compliance with these regulations. Standards such as the General Data

Protection Regulation (GDPR) mandate the protection of personal data through robust security measures, including encryption. Failure to comply with these regulations can result in severe penalties, so encryption is not only a security imperative, but also a legal necessity.

Challenges and Considerations:
While encryption is a powerful tool in the cybersecurity arsenal, its implementation is not without challenges. Key considerations are key management, ensuring secure key distribution, and balancing the trade-off between security and performance. The advent of quantum computers poses a potential threat to traditional encryption algorithms, necessitating the exploration of quantum-resistant encryption methods.

Future trends in encryption:
As technology advances, so does the field of cyber security. The future of encryption is likely to see innovations such as homomorphic encryption, which allows computations on encrypted data without decrypting it. Additionally, advances in

post-quantum cryptography are focused on addressing the looming threat posed by quantum computing.

Encryption technologies are the cornerstone of cybersecurity solutions and provide a robust defense against a myriad of threats. From data protection and secure communications to regulatory compliance and insider threat mitigation, encryption applications are diverse and indispensable. As the digital landscape continues to evolve, encryption technologies must also evolve to adapt to new challenges and ensure the continued resilience of cybersecurity measures.

3.4 Multi-Factor Authentication (MFA)

In an era dominated by digital interactions and the widespread integration of technology into everyday life, the need for robust cybersecurity measures is more pronounced than ever. As cyber threats continue to evolve, protecting sensitive information has become a top concern for individuals and organizations alike. One of the essential tools in the cybersecurity arsenal is Multi-Factor Authentication

(MFA), a security mechanism that adds another layer of protection beyond traditional username and password combinations. In this comprehensive survey, we delve into the importance of MFA in protecting digital assets, its underlying principles, implementation strategies, and the evolving cybersecurity landscape.

Understanding the threat landscape:

Cyber threats have evolved exponentially over the years, from simple phishing attacks to complex malware and sophisticated social engineering tactics. As traditional authentication methods that rely primarily on usernames and passwords are vulnerable to compromise, the need for a more resilient defense mechanism arises. MFA addresses this vulnerability by requiring users to provide multiple forms of identification before access is granted, greatly increasing the security posture.

Basic principles of multi-factor authentication:

MFA works on the basic principle of "something you know, something you have, and something you are." This approach recognizes that relying on passwords alone is insufficient because they can be easily forgotten, shared, or stolen. By combining multiple factors, MFA mitigates the risk associated with a single point of failure. Factors typically include:

1. Knowledge Factors (something you know): This includes traditional credentials such as passwords or PINs.
2. Ownership factors (something you have): These include physical devices such as smartphones, smart cards or tokens.
3. Biometric factors (something you are): Using unique biological characteristics such as fingerprints, facial recognition or retinal scans.

By combining these factors, MFA creates a formidable barrier against unauthorized access, greatly reducing the likelihood of an unauthorized breach.

Implementation strategy for MFA

1. Two Factor Authentication (2FA):

- 2FA is the most basic form of MFA, requiring users to provide two different types of identification before accessing the system.

- Common examples include receiving a one-time code on a mobile device or using a smart card in conjunction with a password.

2. Biometric Authentication:

- Biometric authentication uses unique biological characteristics and provides a high level of security and user convenience.

- Fingerprint scanning, facial recognition and iris scanning are widely used to verify the identity of users.

3. Time-Based One Time Passwords (TOTP):

- TOTP involves generating temporary passwords that are valid for a short period of time.

– Users typically receive these time-sensitive codes through mobile apps such as Google Authenticator or receive them via SMS.

4. Hardware Tokens:

- Hardware tokens, such as USB security keys, generate authentication codes and serve as a physical ownership factor.

- These tokens add another layer of security as they are not susceptible to phishing attacks.

Benefits of an MFA in Cyber Security

1. Enhanced Security: MFA greatly reduces the risk of unauthorized access, even if passwords are cracked.

2. User Responsibility: Users are more responsible for their actions because access requires multiple forms of identification.

3. Compliance Requirements: Many regulatory frameworks mandate the implementation of MFA to meet strict safety standards.

4. Adaptability: MFA is adaptable to different platforms, applications and industries, making it a versatile solution.

Challenges and considerations:

While MFA offers significant benefits, its implementation is not without challenges.

Organizations must consider factors such as user experience, compatibility with existing systems, and the potential for increased support overhead. Achieving a balance between security and usability is critical to ensuring successful MFA adoption.

The Evolving Cyber Security Threat Landscape:
As technology advances, so do the tactics used by cybercriminals. The dynamic nature of cyber threats requires continuous improvement of security measures. Once considered a robust solution, MFA faces the challenges of increasingly sophisticated attacks. Advances in artificial intelligence and machine learning allow cybercriminals to target vulnerabilities in MFA systems. As a result, cybersecurity professionals are exploring adaptive authentication methods and risk-based approaches to stay ahead of evolving threats.

Future trends in multi-factor authentication

1. Behavioral Biometrics: Analyzing user behavior such as typing patterns and mouse movements adds another layer of authentication.

2. Zero Trust Security Model: This model assumes that no user or system, even if authenticated, should be trusted, requiring constant authentication.

3. **Biometric Innovations:** Continued developments in biometric technologies, including vein recognition and gait analysis, offer more secure and convenient authentication methods.

Multi-factor authentication is a cornerstone of cybersecurity and provides an effective defense against unauthorized access and data breaches. Its evolution from a supplementary security measure to a standard practice reflects the escalation of threats and the need for proactive defense mechanisms. As organizations and individuals navigate the digital landscape, implementing MFA serves as a critical step in strengthening the security of sensitive information. Embracing MFA principles along with a progressive approach to emerging technologies is critical to staying one step ahead in the eternal cat-and-mouse game of cyber threats.

3.5 Security Information and Event Management (SIEM)

In an ever-evolving cybersecurity landscape, organizations face an increasing number of threats that can compromise sensitive data, disrupt operations, and undermine stakeholder trust. To navigate this complex environment, businesses are turning to sophisticated tools and technologies, one such cornerstone being Security Information and Event Management (SIEM). This end-to-end solution plays a key role in detecting, responding to and mitigating cyber threats. In this article, we delve into the intricacies of SIEM, exploring its features, benefits, and its critical role in strengthening an organization's cyber defenses.

Understanding SIEM

What is a SIEM?

Security Information and Event Management, SIEM for short, is a holistic approach to cyber security that combines Security Information Management (SIM) and Security Event Management (SEM). It involves the collection, analysis and correlation of security data from various sources within the organization's technology infrastructure. These resources can include firewalls, antivirus filters, intrusion detection systems, and more. By aggregating and correlating these data points, a SIEM provides a comprehensive view of an organization's security posture.

How does SIEM work?

SIEM works on the principle of real-time analysis and correlation. Collects log and event data from various systems, applications and network devices across the organization. This data is then normalized and correlated to identify patterns, anomalies and potential security incidents. SIEM tools use predefined rules and algorithms to analyze this data and generate alerts for security professionals when suspicious activity is detected. Continuous SIEM monitoring and analytics enable organizations to respond quickly to emerging threats.

1. Data Collection:

SIEM systems collect vast amounts of data from a variety of sources, including logs, events, and alerts generated by security devices. This data can come from network devices, servers, endpoints and applications.

2. Log Management:

Log management is a key aspect of SIEM that involves the collection, storage and analysis of log data. Logs contain valuable information about system activities, user behavior, and potential security incidents.

3. Event Correlation:

SIEM tools use advanced correlation techniques to connect seemingly unrelated events and identify potential security incidents. This correlation helps distinguish normal activities from suspicious activities.

4. Notification and Incident Response:
When a potential security incident is detected, SIEM systems generate alerts that alert security personnel. These alerts include details about the incident, allowing for a quick and effective response to mitigate the threat.

5. Reporting and Compliance:
SIEM solutions provide comprehensive reporting capabilities that enable organizations to generate reports on security events, incidents and compliance status. This is essential for regulatory requirements and internal auditing.

Benefits of SIEM in cyber security

1. Early detection of threats:
SIEM's real-time monitoring and correlation capabilities allow organizations to detect security threats at an early stage. This proactive approach helps mitigate potential risks before they escalate.

2. Improved incident response:

By providing detailed information about security incidents, SIEM enables security teams to respond quickly and effectively. This reduces the time required to identify, analyze and mitigate threats.

3. Regulatory Compliance:

Many industries have strict regulatory requirements regarding data security. SIEM helps organizations meet these compliance standards by providing the necessary monitoring and reporting tools.

4. Centralized security management:

SIEM serves as a centralized platform for managing and monitoring security events within an organization's IT infrastructure. This centralized approach increases efficiency and simplifies security operations.

5. Improved visibility:

SIEM provides a holistic view of an organization's security environment and helps security professionals understand the relationships between various events and activities. This increased visibility is critical to making informed decisions.

Challenges and considerations

1. Complexity of implementation:
Deploying and configuring a SIEM solution can be complex and resource intensive. Organizations must invest time and effort in setting up the system properly to ensure its effectiveness.

2. Warning overload:
SIEM systems can generate a large number of alerts, and distinguishing between false positives and real threats can be challenging. Proper tuning and fit are critical to reducing wakefulness fatigue.

3. Skill Requirements:
Effective use of SIEM tools requires experienced professionals who can interpret and respond to the information provided by the system. Continuous training and development are critical to the success of SIEM implementations.

4. The Evolving Threat Landscape:
Cyber threats are constantly evolving and SIEM solutions must adapt to new attack vectors and techniques. Regular updates and ongoing monitoring are essential to ensure the effectiveness of a SIEM system against emerging threats.

Future trends in SIEM

1. Integration with Artificial Intelligence (AI) and Machine Learning (ML):
The integration of AI and ML technologies increases the capabilities of SIEM systems. These technologies enable more advanced threat detection and reduce false positives by learning from historical data.

2. Cloud integration:
As organizations increasingly migrate their infrastructure to the cloud, SIEM solutions are evolving to provide seamless integration with cloud environments. This ensures comprehensive security coverage for both on-premise and cloud assets.

3. User and Entity Behavior Analysis (UEBA):

SIEM systems include UEBA to analyze and understand the behavior of users and entities within the network. This helps in identifying insider threats and detecting abnormal activities that may indicate a security breach.

Security Information and Event Management (SIEM) is a critical part of a cybersecurity solution. Its ability to collect, analyze and correlate vast amounts of security data provides organizations with the means to effectively detect and respond to threats. Despite the challenges associated with implementation and ongoing management, the benefits of early threat detection, improved incident response, and compliance make SIEM an indispensable tool for protecting sensitive information in today's digital environment. As the cybersecurity landscape continues to evolve, SIEM is likely to play an even more important role, adapting to emerging threats and technologies to provide robust protection for organizations worldwide.

3.6 Endpoint Security

Endpoint security is a critical part of a comprehensive cybersecurity solution that protects the vital points where devices connect to the network. In an ever-evolving cyber threat landscape, organizations must prioritize protecting endpoints such as computers, smartphones, and other devices to prevent unauthorized access, data breaches, and other malicious activities.

One of the primary goals of endpoint security is to detect, prevent, and respond to potential security threats at the device level. As cyber attackers continue to refine their tactics, endpoint security solutions play a key role in staying ahead of these threats. Traditional antivirus software, while still necessary, is no longer sufficient by itself. Endpoint security takes a more holistic approach, considers different attack vectors, and uses advanced techniques to harden endpoints.

The rise of remote work has intensified the need for robust endpoint security. With employees accessing sensitive data from multiple locations and devices, the attack surface has expanded, making endpoints more vulnerable. A comprehensive endpoint security strategy includes a variety of technologies and practices, including antivirus software, firewalls, intrusion detection systems, and endpoint detection and response (EDR) solutions.

Antivirus software remains an essential part of endpoint security, scanning files and monitoring activity on devices to identify and remove malicious code. However, modern endpoint security solutions go beyond traditional antivirus measures. They use artificial intelligence and machine learning algorithms to detect previously unknown threats based on behavioral patterns, helping to identify and mitigate zero-day attacks.

Firewalls play a key role in endpoint security by monitoring and controlling incoming and outgoing network traffic based on predefined security rules. This ensures that only authorized connections are allowed, preventing unauthorized access and potential breaches. Firewalls are essential not only for traditional office environments, but also for remote work scenarios where devices connect to different networks.

Another important part of endpoint security is intrusion detection systems (IDS). These systems actively monitor network and/or system activity for malicious behavior or policy violations. When suspicious activity is detected, the IDS will trigger alerts or take proactive measures to avert potential threats. This real-time monitoring is essential to quickly identify and respond to security incidents.

Endpoint detection and response (EDR) solutions provide an additional layer of defense by continuously monitoring and analyzing endpoint activities. EDR goes beyond traditional antivirus measures by offering real-time visibility into endpoint events, enabling security teams to more effectively investigate and respond to incidents. This proactive approach is critical to identifying and mitigating advanced threats before they can cause significant damage.

One of the key challenges in endpoint security is the sheer variety of devices and operating systems in use today. From Windows and macOS to iOS and Android, organizations must secure a large number of endpoints with varying security requirements. An endpoint security solution must be versatile and capable of providing consistent protection in this heterogeneous environment.

As cyber threats become more sophisticated, endpoint security must evolve accordingly. Threat intelligence feeds that provide real-time information on the latest cyber threats and vulnerabilities are integral to improving endpoint security. By leveraging threat intelligence, organizations can proactively update their security measures to defend against emerging threats.

User awareness and training are critical elements of any effective endpoint security strategy. Phishing attacks, which often target individuals through fraudulent emails or messages, continue to be a prevalent threat. Educating users about the risks and tactics used by cybercriminals can significantly reduce the likelihood that they will become victims of such attacks.

Endpoint security is not a one-size-fits-all solution. Organizations must tailor their approach based on their specific needs, industry regulations and the nature of their operations. Regular security assessments and audits help ensure endpoint security measures remain effective and up-to-date in the face of evolving threats.

Endpoint security is the cornerstone of modern cyber security solutions. As technology advances and cyber threats become more sophisticated, organizations must prioritize endpoint protection to protect sensitive data and prevent unauthorized access. A comprehensive endpoint security strategy, including antivirus software, firewalls, intrusion detection systems, EDR solutions, threat intelligence and user training, is essential to creating a resilient defense against the ever-evolving cyber threat landscape.

3.7 Network Security Solutions

Network security solutions play a key role in protecting an organization's digital assets from the ever-evolving cyber threat landscape. As cyber attacks become more sophisticated and widespread, businesses need robust cybersecurity solutions to protect their networks, data and systems. In this comprehensive survey, we delve into the importance of network security solutions in the broader context of cyber security.

Introduction to Network Security Solutions:
Network security solutions include a range of technologies, processes and practices designed to protect the computer network infrastructure from unauthorized access, misuse, modification or denial of service. These solutions are an integral part of an organization's cybersecurity strategy to create a secure and resilient digital environment.

Key components of a network security solution

1. Firewalls:
Firewalls act as the first line of defense by monitoring and controlling incoming and outgoing network traffic. They create a barrier between a secure internal network and external networks, preventing unauthorized access and potential cyber threats.

2. Intrusion Detection and Prevention Systems (IDPS):

IDPS are key to identifying and mitigating potential security threats in real time. They analyze network and system activities, detect anomalies or malicious behavior, and take preventive measures to protect the network.

3. Virtual Private Networks (VPN):

VPNs ensure secure communication over the Internet by encrypting data transmitted between remote users and the corporate network. This is necessary to maintain the confidentiality and integrity of sensitive information, especially when working remotely.

4. Anti-virus and anti-malware software:

These solutions are designed to detect, prevent and remove malicious software such as viruses, worms and spyware from computer systems. Regular updates are essential to stay ahead of emerging threats.

5. Network Access Control (NAC):

NAC regulates network access based on a user's identity and the security status of their device. It ensures that only authorized and compliant devices can connect to the network, reducing the risk of unauthorized access.

6. Security Information and Event Management (SIEM):

SIEM solutions aggregate and analyze log data from various systems in a network. They provide real-time visibility into security events and help organizations quickly detect and respond to potential threats.

Network Security Challenges

Despite advances in network security solutions, organizations face several challenges in maintaining a robust cybersecurity posture:

1. Advanced Persistent Threats (APT):

APTs are sophisticated and targeted attacks that aim to gain unauthorized access to a network for an extended period of time. Detecting and mitigating APTs requires advanced security measures and constant vigilance.

2. Zero-Day Exploits:

A zero-day exploits targeted vulnerabilities in software that are unknown to the vendor. As a result, traditional security measures may be ineffective against these attacks, highlighting the need for proactive security strategies.

3. Insider Threats:

Malicious or unintentional actions by internal users pose a significant threat to network security. Organizations must implement measures to monitor and mitigate the risks associated with insider threats.

4. IoT Security:

The proliferation of Internet of Things (IoT) devices brings new vulnerabilities. Network security solutions must adapt to the challenges posed by the growing number of interconnected devices.

Emerging trends in network security solutions

1. Zero Trust Security Model:

The Zero Trust model works on the principle of "never trust, always verify". It assumes that threats can exist both outside and inside the network, emphasizing the constant authentication of users and devices.

2. Artificial Intelligence and Machine Learning:

Artificial intelligence and machine learning are integrated into network security solutions to improve threat detection and response capabilities. These technologies enable faster and more accurate identification of suspicious activities.

3. Edge Computing Security:

With the advent of edge computing, the security of decentralized networks and data processing at the edge is becoming essential. Network security solutions must extend their protection measures to these distributed environments.

4. Cloud Security:

As organizations use cloud services, ensuring the security of data stored and processed in the cloud becomes paramount. Cloud network security solutions provide scalable and flexible protection for distributed infrastructures.

The importance of network security in cyber security

1. Data protection:

Network security solutions play a vital role in protecting sensitive data from unauthorized access and potential breaches. Encryption, secure transport protocols and access control contribute to robust data protection.

2. Continuity of business:

Cyber attacks can disrupt normal business operations, leading to financial losses and reputational damage. Network security solutions, through measures such as disaster recovery planning, help maintain business continuity in the face of cyber threats.

3. Regulatory Compliance:

Many industries are subject to strict data protection regulations. Network security solutions help organizations comply with these regulations by implementing measures such as data encryption, access control and audit trails.

4. Customer Trust:

A strong commitment to cyber security, supported by effective network security solutions, increases customer confidence. Clients and partners are more likely to engage with organizations that prioritize the protection of their sensitive information.

Best practices for implementing network security solutions

1. Risk assessment:

Conduct regular risk assessments to identify potential vulnerabilities and threats to the network. This helps in developing a targeted and effective network security strategy.

2. Employee training:

Human error is a common factor in security breaches. Regular training and awareness programs educate employees on cybersecurity best practices and make them less likely to fall victim to social engineering or phishing attacks.

3. Correction Management:

Keep your software and systems up to date with the latest security patches. Timely patching is essential to address known vulnerabilities and prevent exploitation by cybercriminals.

4. Incident Response Plan:

Develop and regularly update an incident response plan to ensure a rapid and coordinated response to security incidents. This includes steps for containment, eradication and recovery.

Network security solutions are an integral part of the broader cyber security landscape and serve as the frontline defense against a myriad of cyber threats. As technology advances, organizations must evolve their network security strategies to stay ahead of sophisticated adversaries. By embracing innovative technologies, adopting a proactive security mindset, and following best practices, businesses can create a resilient and secure network infrastructure in the face of an ever-changing threat landscape.

Chapter 4. Best Practices for Implementing Cybersecurity

In an increasingly connected world, the importance of robust cybersecurity practices cannot be overstated. As organizations navigate a complex digital landscape, implementing effective cybersecurity solutions is paramount to protecting sensitive information, maintaining business continuity, and maintaining stakeholder trust. This article covers comprehensive best practices for implementing a cybersecurity solution, covering key aspects such as risk assessment, strategic planning, employee education, and technology integration.

I. Understanding the Cyber Security Environment:

A. Risk assessment:

1. Conduct a thorough risk assessment to identify potential vulnerabilities and threats specific to your organization.

2. Prioritize risks based on their potential impact and likelihood to ensure a targeted approach to cybersecurity implementation.

3. Reassess risks regularly to adapt to evolving cyber threats and technological advances.

B. Regulatory Compliance:

1. Stay informed about relevant cybersecurity regulations and compliance standards.

2. Ensure your cybersecurity strategy aligns with industry compliance requirements.

3. Establish processes for ongoing monitoring and reporting.

II. Strategic planning:

A. Develop a cybersecurity strategy:

1. Formulate a comprehensive cybersecurity strategy that aligns with your organization's overall business goals.

2. Clearly define roles and responsibilities within the cybersecurity team to ensure effective implementation.

3. Establish key performance indicators (KPIs) to measure the success of your cybersecurity initiatives.

B. Incident Response Plan:

1. Develop a detailed incident response plan that outlines the steps to take in the event of a cybersecurity incident.

2. Regularly test and update the incident response plan to reflect changes in technology and potential threats.

3. Train employees in their roles during a cyber security incident to minimize response time.

III. Education and awareness of employees:

A. Cyber Security Training:

1. Provide regular cybersecurity training for all employees to increase their awareness of potential threats.

2. Tailor training programs to address specific risks associated with job roles and responsibilities.

3. Foster a culture of cybersecurity awareness and responsibility throughout the organization.

B. Phishing Awareness:

1. Educate employees on recognizing and avoiding phishing attempts.

2. Implement simulated phishing exercises to assess and improve employees' ability to identify potential threats.

3. Create a reporting system for employees to report suspicious emails and incidents.

IV. Technology integration:

A. Endpoint Security:

1. Deploy a robust endpoint security solution to protect devices connected to the organization's network.

2. Regularly update and patch software to address vulnerabilities and improve security.

3. Implement device management policies to secure company-owned and bring-your-own-device (BYOD) environments.

B. Network Security:

1. Use firewalls, intrusion detection/prevention systems, and a secure network architecture to protect against external threats.

2. Use virtual private networks (VPNs) to secure remote connections and data transfers.

3. Conduct regular security audits to identify and address vulnerabilities in the network infrastructure.

C. Data Protection:

1. Encrypt sensitive data to protect it from unauthorized access.

2. Implement access controls and regularly review user permissions to prevent data leakage.

3. Back up important data regularly and test the recovery process to ensure data resilience.

Implementing a cybersecurity solution requires a multifaceted approach that includes risk assessment, strategic planning, employee education, and technology integration. By adopting these best practices, organizations can strengthen their defenses against evolving cyber threats and cultivate a resilient cybersecurity posture. As the digital landscape continues to evolve, remaining proactive and committed to cybersecurity best practices is critical to maintaining stakeholder trust and protecting the integrity of organizational assets.

4.1 Cybersecurity Frameworks and Standards

In a rapidly evolving digital environment, the importance of robust cybersecurity measures cannot be overstated. Cyber threats continue to grow in sophistication and frequency, posing significant challenges to individuals, organizations and governments around the world. To address this escalating threat landscape, cybersecurity frameworks and standards have emerged as key tools for designing, implementing, and managing effective cybersecurity solutions.

Understanding Cyber Security Frameworks:

The Cybersecurity Framework serves as a comprehensive guide that provides a structured approach to managing and improving an organization's cybersecurity posture. One of the most widely used frameworks is the National Institute of Standards and Technology (NIST) Cybersecurity Framework. It consists of five basic functions: Identification, Protection, Detection, React and Recovery.

- Identification: This phase involves understanding and managing cyber security risks, including asset management, business environment, governance and risk assessment.

- Protect: This is where organizations implement safeguards to ensure the delivery of critical services, including access control, awareness training and data protection measures.

- Detection: Emphasis is placed on early identification of cybersecurity events, including continuous monitoring, anomaly detection, and incident response capabilities.

- Response: In the event of a cyber security incident, organizations must have response plans in place, including communication strategies, mitigation measures and coordination with relevant stakeholders.

- Recovery: After an incident, the organization must recover and improve its capabilities, learn from the experience and improve future resilience.

Importance of Cyber Security Standards:
Cybersecurity standards complement the frameworks by offering specific, detailed requirements and best practices. The International Organization for Standardization (ISO) and the International Electrotechnical Commission (IEC) are working together to develop ISO/IEC 27001, a globally recognized information security management system (ISMS) standard.

- Risk Management: ISO/IEC 27001 emphasizes a risk-based approach that helps organizations systematically identify, assess and manage information security risks.

- Continuous Improvement: Implementation standards support a culture of continuous improvement and ensure that cybersecurity measures evolve to address emerging threats and vulnerabilities.

- Global Consistency: Adherence to recognized standards provides a common language for cybersecurity across borders, facilitating international collaboration and information sharing.

Framework and Standards in Action:

The real power of cybersecurity frameworks and standards lies in their practical application. Consider a scenario where a financial institution is strengthening its cybersecurity defenses.

- Identification: The institution conducts a thorough assessment of its assets, identifies critical financial systems and evaluates potential cyber risks to its operations.

- Protection: Access controls are improved, encryption is implemented for sensitive data and employee training programs are intensified to increase awareness of phishing threats.

- Detection: Continuous monitoring tools are deployed to detect anomalies in network traffic and intrusion detection systems are set to immediately identify any unauthorized access attempts.

- Response: In the unfortunate event of a cyber incident, the institution follows a predefined incident response plan that includes isolating affected systems, informing stakeholders, and coordinating with law enforcement if necessary.

- Recovery: After an incident, the institution focuses on restoring services, learning from the incident to improve future response capabilities, and implementing changes to prevent recurrence.

Challenges and future trends:

While cybersecurity frameworks and standards have greatly improved digital resilience, challenges remain. Rapid technological advances, increasing connectivity, and the rise of sophisticated cyber threats require constant adaptation.

- Agility:An organization must balance the need for security with the agility required to adopt new technologies. Cybersecurity frameworks should be flexible enough to accommodate evolving digital environments.

- Global collaboration: The interconnectedness of the digital world requires global collaboration. Cybersecurity frameworks and standards should promote international cooperation to effectively combat cross-border cyber threats.

- Evolving Technologies: As artificial intelligence, the Internet of Things, and cloud computing expand, cybersecurity frameworks must evolve to address the unique challenges these technologies present.

Cybersecurity frameworks and standards play a key role in strengthening the digital landscape against an ever-expanding array of cyber threats. By providing a structured approach and concrete guidance, these frameworks and standards enable organizations to systematically improve their cybersecurity posture. As the digital ecosystem continues to evolve, continuous refinement and global collaboration around cybersecurity frameworks and standards will be essential to ensure the integrity, confidentiality and availability of digital assets.

4.2 Risk Assessment and Management

Risk assessment and management are critical components of a cybersecurity solution and play a key role in protecting organizations from the ever-evolving cyber threat landscape. As digital transformation accelerates, businesses are increasingly dependent on technology, making them more vulnerable to cyber attacks. This contextual content explores the importance of risk assessment and management in cyber security solutions, delving into their principles, methodologies and their practical implementation.

In the dynamic field of cybersecurity, understanding and mitigating risk is paramount to the success of any organization's digital strategy. Cyber threats continue to evolve in sophistication, from ransomware attacks to data breaches, highlighting the need for a robust risk assessment and management framework.

Cyber Security Risk Assessment:
Risk assessment in cyber security involves identifying, evaluating and prioritizing potential threats to an organization's information systems. It is a proactive process that seeks to anticipate and understand vulnerabilities, enabling organizations to develop effective strategies to mitigate potential risks.

Property identification:
The first step in risk assessment is the identification and classification of digital assets. This includes

sensitive data, software, hardware and network infrastructure. Understanding the value of each asset is critical to determining the potential impact of a security breach.

Threat Identification:
Once the assets are identified, the next step is to assess the potential threats. Threats can range from external sources such as hackers and malware to internal risks such as human error or system failure. A comprehensive threat identification process ensures that organizations are aware of the diverse range of risks they may face.

Vulnerability Assessment:
Conducting a vulnerability assessment involves identifying weaknesses in an organization's security infrastructure. This includes examining software vulnerabilities, outdated security protocols, and potential entry points for cybercriminals. Addressing these vulnerabilities is critical to building a resilient cybersecurity posture.

Risk Analysis:

After identifying threats and vulnerabilities, a risk analysis is performed to quantify the potential impact and probability of occurrence of these risks. This process allows organizations to prioritize their efforts and focus on the most critical threats that could seriously impact their operations.

Cybersecurity Risk Management:

Risk management involves the development and implementation of strategies to mitigate, transfer or accept identified risks. It is a holistic approach that goes beyond mere risk identification and analysis to create a proactive and adaptive security posture.

Risk mitigation strategies:

Organizations implement various strategies to mitigate identified risks. This can include deploying advanced cybersecurity technologies, implementing secure coding practices, and implementing robust access controls. Encryption, firewalls, and intrusion detection systems are examples of tools used to mitigate specific risks.

Incident Response Planning:

In addition to preventive measures, organizations must develop incident response plans to effectively manage and recover from security incidents. Timely and coordinated responses to cyber threats can minimize the impact and downtime caused by a security breach.

Continuous monitoring and improvement:

The field of cybersecurity is constantly evolving, requiring organizations to adopt a continuous monitoring approach. Regularly evaluating and updating security measures ensures that the organization remains resilient to emerging threats. Continuous improvement is the basis of effective risk management.

Practical implementation:

Implementing a robust risk assessment and management framework involves collaboration between different departments within the organization. It requires leadership commitment, adequate resources and a culture of cybersecurity awareness among employees.

Involvement in leadership:

Leadership plays a key role in creating a cybersecurity culture within an organization. Executives must be actively involved in setting priorities, allocating resources, and communicating the importance of cybersecurity to all employees.

Employee training and awareness:

Human error remains a significant factor in many cybersecurity incidents. Providing regular training and awareness programs ensures that employees understand their role in maintaining a secure digital environment. This includes recognizing phishing attempts, using secure passwords, and reporting suspicious activity.

Integration with business processes:

A successful risk management strategy is integrated into the organization's overall business processes. It should align with the goals and objectives of the organization and ensure that cyber security is not seen as a separate entity but as an integral part of the business strategy.

Effective risk assessment and management are essential elements of a robust cyber security solution. Organizations must constantly adapt to the evolving threat landscape and adopt a proactive approach to identifying, analyzing and mitigating risks. Integrating risk management into the fabric of an organization's culture ensures a resilient cybersecurity posture, protects sensitive information, and maintains stakeholder trust in an increasingly connected digital world.

4.3 Employee Training and Awareness

In an ever-evolving technology landscape, businesses are increasingly dependent on digital platforms and networks. While this technological advancement brings a number of benefits, it also exposes organizations to a higher risk of cyber threats. Cybersecurity has become a critical issue for businesses of all sizes, and one of the weakest links in an organization's defense against cyber threats is often its own employees. Recognizing the importance of this human element, organizations are investing in comprehensive employee training and awareness programs to strengthen their cybersecurity posture.

The human factor in cyber security:
The traditional view of cyber security often focuses on sophisticated technological solutions and robust infrastructure. No matter how advanced the technology, the human factor remains a critical aspect of any organization's security framework. Employees, whether intentionally or unintentionally, can become carriers of cyber threats, so it is essential to educate and empower them to be the first line of defense against cyber attacks.

Understanding the Risks:
A comprehensive employee training program begins with creating awareness of the diverse array of cyber risks that organizations face. From phishing attacks to ransomware and social engineering tactics, employees need to be aware of the various methods cybercriminals use to gain unauthorized access or compromise sensitive information. By understanding the risks, employees

can make informed decisions and take a vigilant approach to their digital interactions.

Tailored training programs:
Every organization is unique, as are its cybersecurity needs. Tailoring training programs to address the specific risks and challenges an organization faces increases the relevance and effectiveness of training. Training modules can cover topics such as password hygiene, secure communication practices, identifying phishing attempts and recognizing suspicious activity. Alignment ensures that employees receive training that aligns with the organization's cybersecurity policies and industry-specific threats.

Interactive learning approaches:
Static, monotonous training is less likely to engage employees and may result in limited retention of important information. The use of interactive learning approaches such as simulations, workshops, and real-world scenarios can significantly increase the effectiveness of cybersecurity training. Interactive learning not only

reinforces knowledge, but also provides hands-on experience in dealing with potential cyber threats.

Culture of continuous learning:
Cyber security is a dynamic field where new threats emerge regularly. Therefore, it is essential to adopt a culture of continuous learning to stay ahead of cyber threats. Organizations should encourage employees to stay up-to-date on the latest cybersecurity trends, attend regular training and participate in ongoing awareness programs. This proactive approach ensures that employees remain vigilant and adaptable to evolving cyber threats.

Building a safety-conscious culture:
In addition to formal training, organizations must foster a safety-focused culture among their employees. This includes instilling a sense of responsibility among employees to protect digital assets. Encouraging open communication about security issues, prompt reporting of suspicious activity, and emphasizing shared responsibility for cybersecurity contribute to the development of a robust security culture.

Measuring and evaluating training effectiveness:

In order to measure the success of employee training programs, an organization must establish metrics to measure effectiveness. This may include assessing the frequency of security incidents, the ability of employees to identify and respond to threats, and the overall improvement of the organization's cybersecurity. Regular assessments allow organizations to identify areas for improvement and adjust their training strategies accordingly.

Collaboration with IT and Security Teams:

Employee training should not exist in isolation, but should be integrated into a broader cybersecurity strategy. Close collaboration between IT and security teams and employees ensures that training is aligned with the organization's overall security goals. IT and security teams can provide valuable insights into emerging threats and help tailor training programs to address specific vulnerabilities.

Compliance and Regulatory Aspects:

Many industries are subject to regulations and compliance standards related to cybersecurity. Employee training programs should be consistent with these requirements to ensure that organizations continue to comply with the relevant regulations. This not only helps avoid legal ramifications, but also creates a foundation for cybersecurity best practices in the industry.

In the face of escalating cyber threats, organizations must recognize the critical role employee training and awareness plays in mitigating risk. Investing in comprehensive and customized training programs, fostering a culture of cybersecurity awareness, and maintaining a commitment to continuous learning are essential components of a robust cybersecurity strategy. As technology continues to advance, organizations that prioritize the human element in cybersecurity will be better equipped to navigate the complex and ever-changing digital threat landscape.

4.4 Incident Response and Recovery

In the ever-evolving cybersecurity landscape, organizations face a constant barrage of cyber threats, from sophisticated attacks to common vulnerabilities. Businesses use robust security measures to strengthen their defenses, and at the forefront of these measures is an effective incident response and recovery (IR&R) strategy. This end-to-end approach plays a key role in minimizing the impact of security incidents and ensuring a quick return to normality.

Understanding incident response and recovery

Incident Response (IR): Incident Response is the systematic process of identifying, managing and mitigating security incidents. These incidents may include unauthorized access, data breaches, malware infections or any other cyber threats that threaten the confidentiality, integrity or availability of digital assets. An effective IR plan provides a structured framework for managing an incident, eradicating the threat, and restoring normal operations.

Recovery: While Incident Response deals with the immediate consequences of a security incident, Recovery focuses on restoring systems, data and services to their pre-incident state. Recovery efforts are critical to minimizing downtime, financial loss, and reputational damage. It includes not only technical aspects such as system recovery, but also legal, regulatory and communication aspects.

Incident Response and Recovery Components

1. Preparation:

- **Documentation and Training:** A well-prepared organization maintains thorough documentation of its IT infrastructure, critical assets and potential risks. Regular training ensures that the incident response team is equipped with the skills to effectively deal with different scenarios.

- Incident Response Plan (IRP): Developing a detailed IRP is essential. It outlines roles and responsibilities, communication procedures and a step-by-step guide for responding to different types of incidents.

2. Identification:

- Continuous Monitoring: Using continuous monitoring tools and technologies enables organizations to quickly detect unusual activity or potential security breaches.

- Anomaly detection: Implementing anomaly detection mechanisms helps identify deviations from normal behavior and signals the possibility of a security incident.

3. Container:

- **Isolation: Once an incident is identified, containment involves isolating the affected systems to prevent further spread of the threat.

- Network Segmentation: Well-defined network segmentation limits the lateral movement of attackers within the network, aiding containment efforts.

4. Eradication:

- Root Cause Analysis: Understanding the root cause of an incident is critical to preventing future occurrences. This includes a thorough analysis of the incident, including vulnerability assessment and remediation.

5. Renewal:
    - Data Recovery:** Recovering lost or compromised data is a critical aspect of the recovery phase. This may include restoring from backups or using data recovery tools.
- System Reconfiguration: Bringing systems back to a secure state and implementing configuration changes to prevent similar incidents in the future.

6. Post Incident Analysis:
    - Incident Debriefing:** Conducting a comprehensive debriefing allows the incident response team to evaluate the effectiveness of their response and identify areas for improvement.
    - Documenting Lessons Learned: Documenting the lessons learned from each incident contributes to the continuous improvement and refinement of the incident response plan.

The role of technology in incident response and recovery

1. Security Information and Event Management (SIEM): SIEM tools aggregate and analyze log data from various sources, enabling real-time detection of security incidents.

2. Endpoint Detection and Response (EDR): EDR solutions monitor endpoint activities, provide insight into potential threats, and enable rapid response to malicious activity.

3. Incident Response Platforms (IRP): These platforms simplify the incident response process by providing automated workflows, collaboration tools, and centralized incident documentation.

4. Backup and Recovery Solutions: Robust backup solutions ensure availability of critical data for rapid recovery and reduce the impact of data loss incidents.

1. Timeliness: Rapid response is paramount to mitigating the impact of security incidents. Delays in identification and response can escalate the severity of an incident.

2. Coordination: Coordinating efforts across different teams, departments and external stakeholders can be challenging but is essential for an effective response.

3. Resource Constraints: Many organizations face resource constraints, both in terms of personnel and technology, which can hinder their ability to effectively respond to incidents.

Incident response and recovery are the cornerstones of a robust cybersecurity strategy. At a time when cyber threats are constantly evolving, organizations must be proactive in their approach to protecting digital assets. By implementing a well-defined and regularly tested incident response plan, leveraging advanced technologies and fostering a culture of continuous improvement, organizations can increase their resilience to cyber threats and ensure rapid recovery from security incidents. As the digital landscape continues to evolve, the adaptability and effectiveness of incident response and recovery strategies will remain critical to maintaining the integrity and security of digital environments.

4.5 Regular Security Audits and Penetration Testing

Regular security audits and penetration tests play a key role in strengthening cybersecurity solutions and providing organizations with a robust defense against evolving cyber threats. In today's digital environment, where the frequency and sophistication of cyber-attacks continues to escalate, proactive measures are essential to protect sensitive information and maintain stakeholder trust.

Landscape Understanding:

Cybersecurity is an ever-evolving field where malicious actors are constantly developing new techniques to exploit vulnerabilities. Regular security audits are systematic evaluations of an organization's information systems, policies, and procedures to identify weaknesses that could be exploited by cyber adversaries. These audits serve as a comprehensive health check that allows businesses to assess the effectiveness of their security measures and make informed decisions to increase protection.

Role of Penetration Testing:

Penetration testing, often referred to as ethical hacking, is a proactive approach to identifying vulnerabilities in a system by simulating real-world cyber attacks. Unlike security audits, which focus on compliance and compliance, penetration testing seeks to actively exploit vulnerabilities to assess system resilience. This hands-on approach is essential for organizations looking to gain a deeper understanding of their security posture and the potential impact of a cyber breach.

Comprehensive Security Assessment:

Regular security audits and penetration tests work in tandem to provide a comprehensive security assessment. Audits establish a baseline by examining an organization's adherence to security policies, regulatory requirements, and industry best practices. Penetration testing then goes a step further by actively attempting to break established security measures and mimicking the actions of a determined attacker.

Benefits of regular security audits:

1. Risk Identification and Mitigation: Security audits systematically identify and evaluate potential risks, enabling organizations to prioritize and address vulnerabilities before they can be exploited.

2. Ensure Compliance: In industries with strict regulatory requirements, regular security audits ensure compliance with data protection laws, industry standards and contractual obligations.

3. Policy Assessment: Audits assess the effectiveness of security policies and ensure that

they are not only in place, but also practical and in line with the organization's risk tolerance.

4. Cultural awareness: Regular audits promote a cybersecurity culture within the organization and reinforce employee awareness of the importance of security best practices.

Benefits of Penetration Testing:

1. Real-World Simulation: Penetration testing replicates real-world attack scenarios and provides insight into how well an organization's defenses can withstand real cyber threats.

2. Vulnerability Prioritization: By proactively exploiting vulnerabilities, penetration testing helps prioritize remediation efforts based on the severity and potential impact of identified weaknesses.

3. Improving incident response: Penetration testing helps in evaluating the effectiveness of an organization's incident response mechanisms and helps refine and optimize these processes.

4. Improving Security Posture: Continuous penetration testing enables organizations to develop and improve their security posture and stay ahead of emerging threats and attack vectors.

Integration for maximum efficiency:
While both security audits and penetration tests offer unique benefits, their integration is key to creating a robust cybersecurity strategy. Security audits provide a holistic view of an organization's adherence to policies and standards, while penetration testing delves into the practical effectiveness of these measures.

A cyclical approach that combines regular security audits with periodic penetration testing creates dynamic feedback. Insights gained from penetration testing inform areas of focus for subsequent security audits, ensuring that an organization's defenses are continually refined and adapted to the evolving threat landscape.

Challenges and Considerations:

Implementing regular security audits and penetration tests is not without problems. Barriers can include resource constraints, organizational resistance to change, and the rapidly evolving nature of cyber threats. However, investment in these practices is justified by the potential costs and reputational damage associated with a successful cyber attack.

In addition, organizations should recognize the importance of involving qualified professionals in both security audits and penetration tests. Experienced and certified individuals bring a depth of knowledge and skill, ensuring assessments are thorough and reliable.

The synergy between regular security audits and penetration testing forms the backbone of a robust cyber security solution. While security audits build a foundation by assessing adherence to policies and standards, penetration testing takes a proactive approach by simulating real-world cyber threats.

The dynamic nature of cyber threats requires organizations to take a proactive stance. By incorporating these practices into their cybersecurity framework, businesses can identify vulnerabilities, prioritize remediation efforts, and continually improve their security posture. In an era of risk-filled digital environments, a combination of regular security audits and penetration testing is not just best practice, it's a strategic imperative to protect the integrity of information systems and maintain stakeholder trust.

4.6 Collaboration and Information Sharing in the Cybersecurity Community

In an ever-evolving cyber security threat landscape, collaboration and information sharing have become critical components in strengthening defenses against cyber adversaries. The interconnected nature of our digital world requires a collective and proactive approach to address the sophisticated challenges posed by cyber threats. This contextual content explores the importance of collaboration and information sharing within the cybersecurity community and focuses on how these practices contribute to the development and implementation of robust cybersecurity solutions.

Cyber Security Threat Dynamics

Cyber threats have grown in complexity and scope, with threat actors deploying sophisticated techniques to exploit vulnerabilities in various systems. From ransomware attacks targeting critical infrastructure to advanced persistent threats penetrating sensitive networks, the cyber landscape requires a united front to effectively meet these challenges. Traditional stealthy approaches to cyber security are no longer enough; To stay one step ahead of the evolving threat landscape, a collaborative ecosystem is essential.

The Power of Collaboration

Collaboration between cybersecurity professionals, organizations, and government agencies is key to building resilient defenses against cyber threats. By fostering an environment of open communication and shared intelligence, the cybersecurity community can pool resources, knowledge, and expertise. This collaboration enables the community to quickly respond to emerging threats, share best practices, and collectively improve the overall security posture.

Cybersecurity collaboration goes beyond organizational boundaries. Public-private partnerships play a key role in leveraging the strengths of both sectors. Government agencies can provide valuable threat intelligence, regulatory guidance, and support, while private entities contribute innovation, agility, and specific industry insights. Together, they form a formidable alliance against cyber threats and promote a safer digital environment.

Information Sharing as a Safety Catalyst:

Timely and accurate information sharing is the lifeblood of effective cybersecurity cooperation. Threat intelligence, including indicators of compromise (IoC), tactics, techniques and procedures (TTP), enables organizations to proactively defend against potential attacks. Information sharing platforms, both formal and informal, facilitate the exchange of this critical data between trusted partners and support a collective defense strategy.

One notable example of successful information sharing is the establishment of Computer Emergency Response Teams (CERTs) and Information Sharing and Analysis Centers (ISACs). These entities serve as hubs for sharing cyber security information within specific sectors, allowing organizations to stay informed about sector threats and vulnerabilities. For example, Financial Services ISAC allows financial institutions to share threat intelligence, enabling proactive measures to secure the sector.

Overcoming Challenges in Collaboration and Information Sharing:

While collaboration and information sharing is vital, challenges remain. Barriers include concerns about sharing sensitive information, legal and regulatory barriers, and a lack of standardized formats for data exchange. Overcoming these challenges requires a concerted effort by the cybersecurity community, policymakers, and industry stakeholders.

Establishing clear guidelines for sharing information, ensuring legal protection for the entities involved, and developing standardized protocols for data exchange are essential steps. In addition, fostering a culture of trust and transparency among co-workers is critical to removing power and fostering open communication.

The Role of Technology in Facilitating Collaboration:

Technology serves as a means of enabling effective collaboration and information sharing in the field of cybersecurity. Threat intelligence platforms, secure communication channels and automation tools play a key role in streamlining information exchange while maintaining confidentiality. Blockchain technology, with its own security features, holds promise in creating transparent, tamper-proof systems and sharing sensitive threat data.

In addition, artificial intelligence (AI) and machine learning (ML) algorithms contribute to the analysis of large datasets, identifying patterns and anomalies that human analysts might miss. This technology enhancement increases the speed and accuracy of threat detection and response, a critical factor in the dynamic cyber threat landscape.

The future landscape of cyber security cooperation: As technology continues to evolve, the future of cybersecurity collaboration holds exciting possibilities. On the horizon is improved automation, improved mechanisms for sharing threat intelligence, and increased integration of AI-driven solutions. Interrelated global efforts such as the Paris Call for Trust and Security in Cyberspace exemplify international commitment to promote cooperation and responsible behavior in cyberspace.

Collaboration and information sharing are not just buzzwords in the cybersecurity community; they are fundamental pillars supporting the resilience of our digital infrastructure. By breaking down silos, fostering a culture of trust, and leveraging advanced technology, the cybersecurity community can collectively confront and mitigate the ever-evolving threats in the digital realm. In doing so, we are building a safer and more robust foundation for the future of cyberspace.

CONCLUSION

In conclusion, the ever-evolving cybersecurity landscape requires a comprehensive and adaptive approach to protecting digital assets. The cybersecurity solution discussed in this survey exemplifies a multifaceted strategy that includes robust technology measures, proactive risk management, and a resilient human element. By integrating advanced threat detection, encryption protocols and continuous monitoring, organizations can build a formidable defense against a myriad of cyber threats.

Additionally, the emphasis on user education and awareness underscores the key role individuals play in maintaining a safe digital environment. Cybersecurity Solution recognizes that the human factor is both a vulnerability and a strength. Fostering a culture of cybersecurity awareness among employees is an essential part of any effective cybersecurity strategy.

As we look ahead, the cyber threat landscape will undoubtedly continue to evolve and present new challenges and risks. Cyber security solutions therefore promote an ethos of adaptability and encourage organizations to regularly evaluate and update their security protocols. This dynamic approach ensures that the solution remains agile in the face of emerging threats and provides a robust defense against the ever-changing tactics used by cyber adversaries.

Cybersecurity is not a static goal, but an ongoing journey that requires constant innovation and vigilance. The cybersecurity solutions presented in this discourse serve as a blueprint for organizations seeking to strengthen their defenses at a time when digital assets are under constant siege. By adopting a holistic strategy that combines technological advancements, human empowerment and adaptability, businesses can navigate the complex cyber security landscape with resilience and confidence.

ISBN 9798876759566